# Television/Radio News and Minorities

Donald R. Browne, Charles M. Firestone, and Ellen Mickiewicz

*Foreword by Jimmy Carter*

The Aspen Institute

THE
CARTER CENTER
OF EMORY UNIVERSITY

*For additional copies of this report, please contact:*

The Aspen Institute
Publications Office
P.O. Box 222, 109 Houghton Lab Lane
Queenstown, Maryland 21658
(410) 820-5326    Fax: (410) 827-9174

*For all other inquiries, please contact:*

Commission on Radio and Television Policy
DeWitt Wallace Center for Communications and Journalism
Sanford Institute of Public Policy
Box 90241
Duke University
Durham, North Carolina 27708-0241
(919) 684-5027    Fax: (919) 681-8228

Ellen Mickiewicz                    Mimi Choi
*Director*                          *Assistant Director*

OR

The Aspen Institute
Communications and Society Program
1333 New Hampshire Avenue, NW, Suite 1070
Washington, D.C. 20036
(202) 736-5818    Fax: (202) 467-0790

Charles M. Firestone                Katharina Kopp
*Director*                          *Program Associate*
                                    *and Production Editor*

# CONTENTS

*Foreword* by Jimmy Carter .......................................... v

*Preface* by Eduard Sagalaev .......................................... ix

**1.** Introduction ............................................................. 1

**2.** Background Notes ................................................... 13

**3.** Mainstream vs. Separate Programming
for Ethnic Minorities ............................................... 19

**4.** Coverage of Conflict and Ethnic Minorities ............ 31

**5.** Obtaining Information About Ethnic Groups
and Conflict ............................................................. 63

**6.** Recruitment and Training ..................................... 75

**7.** Enforcement Mechanisms ...................................... 85

**8.** Citizens' Groups as Broadcasters ........................ 105

**9.** Who Will Pay, and at What Cost? ......................... 111

**10.** Languages and Perceptions ................................. 117

**11.** An Afterword, or On to the 21st Century ............. 123

*Report of the Working Group* ................................... 135

*Working Group Conference Participants* ............. 153

*Report of the Commission on Radio and Television Policy* ....................................................... 157

*Commission on Radio and Television Policy Members* ................................................................. 171

*About the Authors* ................................................. 175

*Acknowledgments* ................................................. 177

# FOREWORD

## By Jimmy Carter

*39th President of the United States*

In every society there is some degree of ethnic diversity. Although these differences can impact on communities in positive ways, they also can lead to conflict. This is especially true when racial and ethnic issues are tied to contrasting political and economic agendas, which can tear apart the social fabric and undermine the hope and promise of peaceful human existence. We must learn to prevent our differences from turning into strife. In this ongoing struggle, there is a tool that now reaches into private homes and to the farthest corners of our earth: the electronic media.

Television and radio have the unique capacity to speak to the diversities within countries, but that powerful capability carries a responsibility: How can the media systems of ethnically mixed states integrate all groups within their arena, and how can individuals from diverse cultures and traditions find a way to communicate with each other? The question relates to technical issues of when, where, and how to communicate, as well as to complicated political issues. Whose images and whose authority should be communicated on the electronic media? How should the push of one ethnic group to share power with another, or even replace it in power, be treated? How should the sparks of ethnic complaint and conflict be treated by the media so that they do not become incendiary threats to civil society?

For many states in the world, one answer is to use the media to convey the values and policies of the dominant group. That strategy seems the most stable; it keeps other ethnic groups in the position of consumers and, in theory, dampens their demands by denying them voice. However, we have come to realize that this course is both shortsighted and ineffective. Because of their enormous power in today's world, radio and television can play a long-term role in defusing and moderating ethnic tensions.

It was with an eye toward the long-range implications of electronic media coverage that we convened the second meeting of the Commission on Radio and Television Policy in November 1992 in Almaty, Kazakhstan. At that meeting, we addressed the relationship of ethnic minorities to radio and television news. The issues could not have been more timely. Earlier in the year, riots had broken out in Los Angeles, and ethnic conflicts were wracking the Caucasus and Central Asia. Outside the former Soviet Union and the United States, we saw bitter confrontations in Africa, the Middle East, and Europe. Few societies were immune.

Eduard Sagalaev, my cochairman, and I led the meeting in the hall where the Soviet Union had been dissolved. For the participants, there were no easy solutions to the dilemmas of minorities and the electronic media. All agreed that not reporting conflict enables rumor to sweep across tense landscapes. We also agreed that adopting in advance a program of preparation for conflict coverage would help to prevent the dissemination of misinformation or incomplete information. Equally, the participants found that television and radio can help to prevent conflict from occurring by identifying tensions and needs. But this requires media organizations to recruit and advance members of minorities whose insights can expand the outlook of the entire organization. Not all of the participants agreed with all of the recommendations; but each of us from different countries saw radio and television as vital to resolving some of the most deeply divisive strains in the world.

The Commission on Radio and Television Policy was formed with the purpose of developing policy options for critical issues such as these. Its membership is drawn from media and government officials and academic experts from the United States and from each of the republics of the former Soviet Union. In discussing policy, we do not recommend a single course of action or outcome. Rather, we explore many different options and argue the advantages and disadvantages of each. In that way, any society can configure the set of policies that serves its needs, knowing that there are trade-offs in every choice. Before the Commission meets, a working group elaborates the full set of options the Commission is to consider. Both the Commission's report on the Kazakhstan meeting and that of the working group are included in the book.

*Television/Radio News and Minorities* is the second book to issue from Commission meetings. The first, *Television & Elections,* was launched at a press conference at the United Nations in 1992 and distributed to all of its centers worldwide. At this writing, it has been translated into French, Russian, Kazakh, and Ukrainian, and other translations are under way.

# PREFACE

## By Eduard Sagalaev

*President, Moscow Independent Broadcasting Corporation;*
*Chairman, Confederation of Journalists' Unions*

The countries of the socialist camp are taking steps toward a new life—toward the 21st century. At times it is an extraordinarily agonizing path tied to war, bloodshed, shock, and changes in the very foundations and institutions of the state. It is enough to recall the events in October (1993) in Russia, when the confrontation between the Post-Communist parliament and the democratic government led to the armed coup attempt. The whole world, in alarm, watched CNN's live broadcast from Moscow, and thought about the future of this great country, on the brink of catastrophe.

In Russia, the process of creating new, democratic organs of governmental power is beginning, and, as never before, the greatest responsibility rests with communications—and it goes without saying—on television most of all. The fact that President Boris Yeltsin, in his decree on guarantees of access to mass media during elections, referred to the recommendations of our international Commission on Radio and Television Policy, gives me great satisfaction.

People are making their own choices. People are learning to live in a free society, and are developing new laws and rules. It is very important that our Commission help to shorten and ease this difficult path, by promoting a civilized exchange of experiences and ideas for the development of political culture in our governments.

# INTRODUCTION

## A.

When the BBC came on the air in 1938 with its first foreign language broadcast service (Arabic) for overseas listeners, its very first newscast contained an item about the execution by a British Army firing squad of two Palestinian "terrorists" (although that term was not in use then). That broadcast dealt with conflict, as many broadcasts had done earlier and many more were to do later. But it also dealt with ethnic minorities, if one realizes that Palestinians under British occupation, as well as the British themselves, could regard the British as the majority culture in terms of who held power at the time. Still, the British Foreign Office did express reservations over the wisdom of including such an item in the newscast: It might heighten anti-British sentiment among Arabs in general and Palestinians in particular. And it also might reinforce what some Arabs regarded as a common British tendency to consider Arabs and violence as the same.

Today as well, and perhaps more than ever, conflict in its more violent forms may all too easily and too often be regarded as coterminous with ethnic minorities. (In this volume, we follow the definition of "minority" provided by the Working Group on Television News Coverage of Minorities: ethnic and racial groups not constituting a numerical majority within their respective sovereign state, or, in the case of some former Soviet republics, groups that may comprise a majority but lack titular status.) Consider the list: ethnically driven power struggles in parts of the former Soviet Union; looting and fighting, largely involving ethnic minorities, in the streets of Los Angeles; interethnic civil wars in Bosnia, Sri Lanka, and Sudan; bombs planted by ethnic minority and majority "terrorist" groups in Spain, India, and elsewhere. Members of minority groups certainly may have initiated some of those conflicts, but they have been victims at least as often. However, the experiences of certain multiethnic and multiracial societies— Singapore, Mauritius, the Netherlands, New Zealand— show us that violent conflict and ethnic minorities need not be coterminous.

Still, there is no doubt that conflict and tension, quite often involving ethnic minorities, are very attractive to the mass media in general and the electronic media in particular. That is true not only for newscasts, interviews, talk shows, and documentaries, but also for most entertainment programming, whether situation comedies, dramas, quiz shows, soap operas, or the newer hybrid forms: "dramedies" (drama/situation comedy), "docudramas" (variable mixtures of documentary and drama), or reality-based programs (variable mixtures of footage of real events and recreated and fabricated material related to those events).

As television sets are a virtually universal household fixture in most industrially developed nations, and are growing rapidly in many other nations, it is safe to conclude that the majority of the world's population is exposed to much more conflict, more frequently, and more graphically, than has ever been the case before. That majority is certain to grow in the years ahead. That alone justifies the careful consideration of how television treats conflict and ethnic minorities, whether those considering it are decision makers within the electronic media, governments licensing

2

those media, or those members of the public who may be concerned over seemingly rising levels of mistrust and conflict within multiethnic societies, and seek to discover causes and cures for that condition.

Like its predecessor, *Television & Elections,* this short book treats a single subject. Unlike it, the subject this time is double-headed. That will become evident as the reader comes across sections which treat conflict and ethnic minority issues together, and sections where one or the other has the stage to itself, although what is covered in such sections usually has implications for both.

Also, this book provides a less clear-cut "menu" of varying practices from one television system to another. It presents many categories and specific examples of television's (and sometimes radio's) coverage of ethnic minorities and conflict. However, the topic under consideration here is considerably more complex, and far less often governed by specific laws and clearly articulated practices, than is TV's coverage of elections. Many electronic media systems specify amounts of time, program formats, etc., for election-related programming. Very few systems treat conflict and ethnic minorities in such a formulaic manner, although several systems (e.g., Great Britain, Australia, and New Zealand) have codified or set informal "watershed hours," usually around 9 PM, before which violence and sexually explicit material (some of it involving minorities) is to be held to a minimum, and after which there can be a somewhat freer treatment of those elements. And many nations ban or severely limit in-store sales of pornographic video cassettes, whether they include ethnic minorities or violent forms of conflict or not.

In *Television & Elections,* the experiences of Third World nations featured quite prominently. They are in shorter supply here. However, readers will encounter ethnic and linguistic minorities—Sami, Ojibwa (Anishinabe),

Ainu—that may be totally unfamiliar to them. All three, and others (Maori in New Zealand, Aborigines in Australia), exist within highly industrialized nations (Norway, Finland, and Sweden for Sami, the United States for Anishinabe, Japan for Ainu); and sometimes they exist under what could be termed Third World conditions. Certainly their experiences are relevant to all nations.

As we shall note in the body of the text, there are reasons for the seemingly scant coverage provided on Third World experiences. The broadcast systems of many of those countries may ignore, misrepresent, or treat casually the problems and demands of their ethnic minorities, even as do systems in many industrialized nations. As far more of the Third World media systems are monopolies, minorities that feel slighted have no place else to turn, at least within the world of the media. Also, many Third World nations, especially in sub-Saharan Africa and in South Asia, find it difficult to identify minorities when every tribal, clan, or extended family grouping is a numerical minority. In still others, there may be some of the trappings of democracy, including provision for specified amounts of airtime for political broadcasts by contending parties, but there may be total or near-total suppression of coverage of ethnic minorities or of conflict, on the grounds that life will be more tranquil if everyone is treated as part of one large, happy family.

The range of practices, problems, and experiences presented here is vast, which should be a good indication that we have yet to discover the ideal way to cover conflict and ethnic minorities. Certainly these pages do not present one. What they do present is a panoply of examples, some of broad utility, others more limited in their applicability. All are practical, in the sense that someone has put them into effect. Unfortunately, the nature of the experiences themselves is such that it is far more difficult for us to determine whether the uses made of broadcasting have had the de-

4

sired effect, assuming that someone actually specified the desired effect. Elections have outcomes, and that may allow us to draw at least tangential or inferential links between those outcomes and the manners in which television presented preelection material. Where violence and ethnic minorities are concerned, there is nothing comparable.

## B.

That overall lack of compelling evidence becomes apparent as soon as one begins to examine the body of research bearing on the presentation of ethnic minorities through the electronic media—most often, television. There are numerous quantitative indicators available: numbers and types of stations serving ethnic minorities; amounts of airtime devoted to minority languages; numbers and sizes of grants and other financial support for minority broadcasting; viewing patterns of ethnic minorities; numbers and types of roles played by minorities in entertainment programming; and (although rarely) depiction of minorities in news and public affairs programs. All of those measures can be very useful in identifying underrepresentation, misrepresentation, etc. However, very few of the studies tell us in quantitative terms whether any effort to improve the images of ethnic minorities actually is bearing fruit.

Qualitative studies of ethnic minorities and television also exist, but very few of them examine the effects of media portrayals of ethnic minorities on majority or minority culture perceptions of those minorities. Such research is complex, time-consuming, costly, and even potentially dangerous, as when majority culture researchers attempt to conduct studies of ethnic minority groups and individuals who are mistrustful of or hostile to the majority culture.

It is much safer to conduct quantitative studies which *may* have qualitative implications, such as counting the

5

numbers of depictions of ethnic minority doctors or lawyers in prime-time entertainment programs. A low depiction rate *may* allow one to conclude that television isn't doing much, through entertainment at any rate, to present minority and majority cultures with role models that might eventually increase the numbers and acceptance of minority doctors and lawyers throughout society. Studies along those lines certainly have produced some useful data; for one thing, they generally reveal that TV underrepresents ethnic minorities in terms of their actual numbers, both in general and within the more professional occupations, but often overrepresents minorities in comic or villain roles, real-life or fictional. But such studies tell one nothing about how the audiences, minority and majority alike, react to the depictions, and thus do not allow us to assess whether they may be contributing to a shift of images—one hopes, in a positive direction—concerning "appropriate" roles for minorities.

## C.

The coverage of conflict, whether it involves ethnic minorities or not, is even less clearly measured (and perhaps measurable) chiefly because of its highly subjective nature. One can count incidents of different kinds and committers of violence depicted on television, as many scholars have done. As just indicated, acts of violence, especially in news reporting, seem disproportionately connected with ethnic minorities. But studies of media coverage of conflict per se are rare, although certain British, Swedish, German, and American scholars have examined TV coverage of certain forms and instances of conflict, some of them centering on ethnic minorities: demonstrations, strikes and other union actions, wars. Those studies generally conclude that television tends to favor governments, law enforcement agencies, businesses, and other elements that represent stability. Furthermore, they tend to show that the underlying causes of conflict of *any* sort rarely receive attention through television.

The reason for the paucity of studies of conflict may lie within the term itself. Conflict seems even more difficult to define than violence, which is difficult enough to pin down. It is so much broader; therefore, incidents of it will be more difficult to count, and the manner of counting is almost certain to come under even more criticism than it has with respect to violence. Quite perversely, conflict appears much like beauty, in that it often is in the eye of the beholder. Nor does it help matters that conflict is well-nigh omnipresent on television—not as universal as the air we breathe, but fairly close!

It is impossible to conceive of a world, or even a nation, without conflict of some sort. In fact, such a situation would be unhealthy for any society. A society without conflict might be called anything from peaceful to boring; it is unlikely to be called dynamic.

Still, the very ubiquity of conflict in the images furnished to us through the electronic media is furnished to us *by* those media. At first blush, that observation appears to be self-evident. However, it is meant to serve as a reminder that those who work in the electronic media can become enmeshed in a daily struggle to create its product—to feed the ever-hungry beast—and the process of doing so can come to resemble the manufacture of cars, chewing gum, or soft drinks. Assembly-line workers don't expect to step back from their labors every now and again to consider the social impact of their product. Electronic media staff often face similar pressures to keep the program assembly line moving, as anyone who has ever visited a newsroom or a production studio, much less worked in one, can attest. Granted, there are daily editorial meetings, script confer-

7

ences, dress rehearsals, and other opportunities for reflection, but much of that activity is devoted to economizing on time, working out production problems, and other considerations that have little or nothing to do with the impact of programs on society. And when those newsrooms or production studios are dominated by members of the majority culture, the possibilities for misrepresentation of conflict involving ethnic minorities are particularly great.

## D.

Much the same observation applies to the issue of stereotyping of ethnic minorities. Majority culture domination often carries with it the power to stereotype. It is in itself a way to maintain power, in fact, because it underlines the ability of those holding power to determine how to portray those who do not. The mass media are ideal vehicles for such portrayals, because they extend throughout society, and frequently serve as trend-setters, taste-makers, labelers, and the raw material for daily conversation. What is more, media staff who come from the majority culture tend to represent its views, often unconsciously. Time is almost always in short supply in media operations, and repetition of stereotypes, whether conscious or unconscious, is a great time-saver. They are familiar to society at large, and thus need little, if any, explanation.

Stereotypes often are presented and discussed in terms of their verbal forms, and these certainly can be very potent. But visual stereotyping can be at least as potent, and perhaps more insidious, in that often it does not proclaim itself as openly. Take, for example, the stereotyping effect of continually showing members of a given visually identifiable minority group in a highly restricted number of settings: engaged in protests, "riots," confrontations with law enforcement officials; selling and consuming drugs,

8

trafficking in prostitution; mourning the loss through death or incarceration of children, family members, religious or political leaders. All of those can make for visually compelling television coverage. Taken collectively, and with little else to offset them, it becomes easy for viewers to think of them as constituting the entire universe of that minority.

It would not be possible to exclude stereotypes from any society, nor would it be desirable to do so. We need a certain level of stereotyping to help us to make better sense and order out of life around us, and to do so economically. This is particularly true where television is readily available, since it provides us with a daily dose of information ranging from events that may have happened in our neighborhoods to events that take place on the other side of the globe, and even in outer space. If we were to be presented with highly detailed accounts which provided a variety of perspectives on each event, we probably would recall even less about each one than we now do—and studies of viewer recall of newscasts show very low figures already.

However, it is vital that media staff continually question their own judgments in the use of stereotypes, particularly where those stereotypes are negative. But because they may not seem negative to members of the majority culture, media staff may need more than just extra time to be able to reflect on what they are portraying; they also may need guidance from members of the groups portrayed, who can point out not only how stereotyping feels to them, but also *why* it feels so. Until that is understood, the lesson is not likely to stick.

In the course of learning why, media staff also may come to understand the resentment felt by those stereotyped when the media cover certain behaviors within groups, ethnic minority and otherwise, and build those into stereotypes to be shared and used by the majority culture. For example, virtually every nation's major language has a number of terms, often slang, employed by members of the majority culture to refer negatively to members of minority cultures. Some of those terms have been in common use for so long that they may have come to seem harmless, at least to members of the majority culture. Media staff should be alert to that possibility, and be careful to avoid them in broadcasts, where their presence is likely to reinforce any feeling that it is perfectly all right for the general public to employ them. And if minorities occasionally "borrow" such terms for use among themselves, it should not be assumed that they would welcome their use by and through the media.

In short, if media staff are to help society to become more tolerant, to have a higher degree of mutual understanding, it will take a great deal of conscious thought, and the time necessary for it. That is asking a lot of the electronic media, where time is so precious. But there is no substitute for it.

## E.

The Working Group for the Commission on Radio and Television Policy has drawn up a set of four general policy goals aimed at implementing or reinforcing certain social values: full participation of ethnic minorities in national life; freedom and independence of the press to report fairly; reinforcement of societies' moral values; and development of greater social stability. The policy goals in particular call for an increase in news programming for, about, and by ethnic minorities. They also stress the need for greater provision of minority perspectives through *majority*-oriented media channels. In both cases, they emphasize, there should be an avoidance of stereotyping.

That is an ambitious undertaking, and the text that follows cannot do this complex subject full justice. It *can* suggest various ways of approaching it, and, in certain instances, can indicate whether certain approaches seem to have succeeded in fulfilling policy goals, although there is far less direct or conclusive evidence of success than one would like to see. That only underlines the need for more research of the "right" (and admittedly expensive) sort, which we hope will be shared among electronic media staff throughout the world so that all of us may better deal with this worldwide problem.

This book generally confines itself to consideration of news and public affairs programming. However, there also is a great deal of evidence available which indicates that many audience members find it difficult to distinguish between factual and fictional material presented through the electronic media, for reasons which we shall consider in the text. Therefore, we make room for a discussion of the possible negative and positive roles of fictional programming in presenting conflict and ethnic minorities to society.

### F.

Throughout the text, the reader will note the frequent use of the terms *broadcast(ing)* and *electronic media*. We employ them interchangeably most of the time, and include cable television, wireless cable, direct broadcast reception from satellites, and stand-alone video within them. For the most part, the newer electronic media—audiocassettes, videocassettes, teletext—come to us through devices (recorders, television sets) closely associated with broadcasting. We may be able to use some of them more flexibly, more individualistically, than we use broadcasting, but the material they convey often owes a great deal to "models" provided by broadcasting. More importantly, that material is the product of an individual—more often, a *group* of individuals—with carefully considered reasons for producing it. Since this book often posits the need for those who

11

prepare messages about ethnic minorities and conflict to exercise greater responsibility in doing so, broadcasters and audio- or videocassette producer/distributors alike should find it relevant, although the sheer magnitude of responsibility may differ from one to the other.

# BACKGROUND NOTES

No one can doubt the impact of television on society. Survey after survey in countries around the world shows that, where the general public is concerned, television is regarded as the most believable of the mass media. People who own TV sets spend on average more time watching TV than on any other leisure activity. Scholars and critics in many countries have called it a "mirror of society." Whether they mean that in a positive or a negative sense, it is an endorsement of television's power and prominence.

Still, anyone who has had the opportunity to watch television in a number of countries around the world will be aware that television is a selective mirror. Whether in the United States, the former Soviet Union, or Sri Lanka, San Marino, or Surinam, there are segments of society which never or rarely appear on the screen, and there are other segments which receive little but negatively stereotypical portrayal. Some critics have claimed that such portrayal, or relative neglect, may lead to outbreaks of violence or may cause violence to worsen, as in the Los Angeles "riots" of 1992, the ongoing struggles between various ethnic groups in the former Soviet Union and in Yugoslavia, or the Hindu clashes with Indian Muslims at various temple sites and in Bombay in 1992 and 1993.

When broadcasting emerged around the world some 60 to 70 years earlier, almost always it was the majority culture that created and operated it. The major exception was the colonial world, where the colonizing powers were in charge of it. Even here, however, they ran it for themselves, largely excluding the cultures of their subjects; thus, they behaved as if they were the majority culture. In a few cases, such as the Soviet Union, and Germany under the Nazis, governments used radio to create a "new" society, where majorities and minorities (if they weren't marginalized or eliminated) would retain some degree of distinctiveness, but would drop certain elements of it as they became "new Soviet men" and "workers for National Socialism."

World War II and the immediate postwar period saw increased attention to various "freedoms" and "universal rights." Sometimes there were specific references to minority rights, most often religious and political. Dealing with ethnic minority rights remained a touchy subject for many sovereign nations, some of which faced potentially divisive domestic situations along those lines. The coming of the Cold War resulted in much of the "free world" and the "communist bloc" acting monolithically, but criticizing each other for neglect or maltreatment of ethnic minorities. If minority groups had the opportunity to present themselves on radio or television, it came through stations owned, operated, and largely or totally controlled by majority cultures, and conformed to the stereotypes and purposes of those cultures.

Where coverage of conflict within society was concerned, there appeared to be very little desire on the part of radio stations to become involved in it, whether it centered on ethnic minorities or not. No one had questioned the need for or the right of stations to cover conflict between nations in strongly dichotomous, "right" versus "wrong" terms. But conflict that erupted *within* society during this period—and strikes involving autoworkers, coal miners, etc. were quite common, as were protests by ethnic minorities over what they saw as prejudicial treatment—received generally brief

14

coverage, almost always through newscast items, when they were covered at all. There also was a decided bias in favor of "the establishment," whether government, business and industry, the military, or other—and that usually excluded ethnic minorities. Unions occasionally made attempts to bargain for airtime, or even to purchase it, but they were largely unsuccessful in obtaining it.

The period running from the late 1960s to the late 1970s saw many ethnic minority groups in industrialized nations becoming more active in "power to the people" movements. Part of that activity took the form of learning how to attract coverage on television, but some groups went further and began to seek licenses to broadcast, either on their own or in combination with other minority groups. Almost all of that activity was confined to radio, since television was far too expensive for most groups, and far fewer TV stations could be licensed. Minority-run radio stations grew quite rapidly in Canada, the United States, and Australia, but more slowly elsewhere. In Italy, labor unions, factory workers, and other groups began to operate their own radio stations in the mid-1970s, thanks to loopholes in the Italian broadcast law, but ethnic minority viewpoints there and elsewhere in Europe received little attention, despite the growing numbers of "guest workers" and immigrants throughout the continent.

Meanwhile, mainstream broadcasting began to reexamine its generally stereotypical presentations of ethnic minorities, and in some cases worked to change them. Public service broadcasting organizations (those supported by annual license fees, government appropriations, audience contributions) in Great Britain, New Zealand, and the United States sometimes set aside blocks of airtime in which minorities could present their viewpoints, their cultures, and problems they faced as minorities. Advertiser-supported stations and networks, particularly in the United

15

States, sometimes responded to the threat of consumer boycotts and negative publicity by broadcasting series with positive roles for ethnic minorities: black doctors, Hispanic lawyers, Arab teachers. Canada and the United States introduced equal employment legislation, which helped to increase the numbers of ethnic minority production personnel, newscasters, etc. As a result, audiences began to see and hear more minority viewpoints, although many of those alternative approaches were available only in larger urban areas.

The period from the late 1970s to the late 1980s saw a marked increase in the authorization of commercial (usually private) broadcasting, especially radio, in much of Europe. Many would-be commercial broadcasters had tried their hands through unauthorized, or "pirate," radio, and sought licenses as soon as the opportunity presented itself. The new Socialist-led government in France made that possible in 1982, resulting in the authorization of several stations operated by and broadcasting to North Africans residing in France. Private radio in most Western European nations was more tightly controlled, with Germany and Switzerland opting for licensing systems that favored creation of commercially oriented stations featuring large amounts of popular music. Norway, Sweden, and Denmark took a very different approach, establishing a system of shared transmitter time (*närradio*) that allowed many groups—religious, political, ethnic minority—to have regularly scheduled blocks of airtime available for their virtually unfettered use. Australia and New Zealand began to finance separate broadcast services for and by Aborigines and Maoris.

As we move into the mid-1990s, some 75 years after the birth of broadcasting in several countries, mainstream, majority-culture-dominated radio and television still prevails over all forms of minority-culture broadcasting by a very wide margin, and many minority cultures remain totally ignored by the electronic media. It is rare to find a country where any minority group receives coverage that is even remotely close to its numerical representation; it is not uncommon to find countries where quite sizable minority groups are virtually invisible. There is still a dominant assumption that one side in a conflict—usually the majority culture's side—is either more in the right or totally right. Alternative viewpoints either receive little attention or come from unlicensed (illegal) or foreign-based broadcast outlets, or possibly through audiocassettes distributed en masse, as happened in Iran in 1980 and in Saudi Arabia in the early 1990s. The consequences of underrepresentation of ethnic minority viewpoints for society as a whole may be uncertain and unpredictable, but few doubt that, on the whole, they will be more negative than positive.

# MAINSTREAM vs. SEPARATE PROGRAMMING FOR ETHNIC MINORITIES

As ethnic minorities seek access to the electronic media, they must ask themselves which audiences they hope to reach and for what purposes. That will enable them to decide which particular channels will best serve their needs. Clearly it would be ideal if they were to have access to all available channels, but in some circumstances that is not possible. In such a case, selection of the most appropriate channel is especially important in maximizing chances of success; it then becomes necessary to weigh the advantages and disadvantages of each.

The most common channel is through the *mainstream service*—whatever the majority of people listen to or view most of the time; whatever is most widely receivable; whatever enjoys the highest level of financial support. By and large, the mainstream service also is regarded as society's most significant common denominator, in terms of the programs that are the subject of everyday discussion, the reference points for illustrations by politicians, religious figures, even the print media—in short, important and perhaps predominant sources of the "glue" that holds society together. In many countries, especially within the Third World, but also throughout much of Eastern Europe, the mainstream service is the *only* service. In others, such as Japan, Australia, the United States, Germany, Italy, and Mexico, there may be several competing national services, but rarely do they differ to any substantial degree in their depictions of society through their factual or fictional programming.

Those competing services may be financed through sales of airtime for advertising, through annual license fees paid by the audience, or through annual appropriations by the legislature, but they have one thing in common: They do not go out of their way to mirror the situations of ethnic minorities, but instead concentrate on the majority culture which purchases most advertised goods, which accounts for the largest percentage of annual license fees, and which pays the lion's shares of the income taxes that are the chief sources of annual appropriations.

Where the depiction of the ongoing daily life of the world is concerned, the chief mainstream services are news and public affairs programs; there, minority viewpoints generally appear as the program producers (usually from the majority culture) think appropriate, with no absolute guarantees of regularly scheduled, recurring amounts of airtime. The advantages to such airtime are that appearing on the mainstream service is likely to provide minorities with relatively large audiences for their appearances, and that the programs themselves will be produced in a "professional" manner by the mainstream service's usual staff.

But there are several disadvantages. If ethnic minorities are numerous, as they are in many African nations and in some parts of the former Soviet Union, mainstream stations probably will spread airtime among them, so as to avoid accusations of bias. Those pieces of airtime are unlikely to provide any one minority with much opportunity to reach the broader public, much less the opportunity of establishing any sense of continuity. For example, the tiny West African nation of Gambia broadcasts in English, Wolof, Mandinke, Fula, and several localized languages, over one radio service which is on the air for roughly 12 hours a day. In Kazakhstan, a mosaic of European and Asian ethnic groups, there are daily broadcasts in a number of local languages, and in much smaller Lithuania, there are broadcasts at least once a month in the Russian, Polish, Belarusian, Ukrainian, Yiddish, Tatar, and Latvian languages. If the minority service is in the particular language of each minority, that may limit its prospects for reaching a broader public, or other minorities. But it *is* important that such languages be heard.

> *The Commission strongly recommended that "when different languages are used by minority members, the total television system should provide programming in the language of the minorities."*

In such circumstances, the public's impression may be of so many snapshots presented more or less randomly. In Germany, for example, the mainstream public radio services (but *not* television) provide 20-minute blocks of airtime each day for Turkish, Italian, and other "guest workers" residing there, but each block is in the language of a given nationality, further reducing its accessibility for the larger public. There is little opportunity—and none on a regularly scheduled basis—for majority culture listeners to learn much about those minorities, especially in the minorities' own terms. However, any marked increase in airtime for or about minorities, in Germany or elsewhere, would be unlikely to find favor in the eyes or ears of the mainstream (majority culture) public. The majority usually is resistant to any pre-emption or displacement of its favorite programs or of the sorts of news coverage it most values, even though more ethnic minority material may be "good" for it.

A related disadvantage (but not always) is that time devoted to news and public affairs programs may be variable, with more made available when there is trouble involving ethnic minorities, but less when things appear to be calm. If the scheduling of material about ethnic minorities varies, as it often does, interested viewers may have no way to predict when they might hear or see such material. That has a potentially positive side: Viewers who consciously or unconsciously try to avoid such material will find it harder to do so when scheduling varies, and may even find themselves watching with interest something that they never would have searched out on their own.

There also may be a problem with mainstream production staff. If, as often is the case, they come from the majority culture, they may not understand ethnic minority cultures, and may not even care to understand them. In extreme circumstances, they may even be hostile toward them. Lacking sensitivity or interest, they may do an insensitive or disinterested job of portraying minorities, ranging from inappropriate questions in interviews to unflattering camera shots. If hostile, they can easily sabotage a production.

Finally, placing ethnic minority material within mainstream programs that contain many other kinds of material virtually requires that minorities present themselves in terms that mainstream viewers can understand—language, terms of reference, even perhaps gestures. That may not be difficult for minority group members, but it may weaken a carefully nurtured sense of identity for the groups themselves, if for example they feel strongly about using their own language to express matters of greatest concern to them.

*Part of the solution may lie in making sure that a variety of journalists cover these issues. The importance of the presence of journalists from both minority and majority groups cover-*

*ing not only specifically ethnic issues but also other subjects was underscored by the Commission. It recommended that "both minority and majority reporters and commmentators report stories about ethnic issues. It is equally important that more general stories be covered by reporters, some of whom are minority citizens."*

There is another type of mainstream programming involving ethnic minorities. Mainstream services may decide to turn over *blocks of airtime* to minority groups, perhaps providing them with studios, equipment, and even production staff, but leaving the editorial decisions up to the groups. That practice is quite rare, since most mainstream services choose to exercise ultimate editorial control through a top official—the head of television news, the director of TV services, even the manager or director general of the entire operation. That individual answers to still other officials, usually governmental, and cannot easily excuse some "offensive" or "misleading" program on the grounds that it was a minority group's responsibility. But it is possible to allow the group considerable editorial freedom, subject to some broad stipulations that set very few practical limits on what it may say or show. Many independent (commercial) local radio (ILR) stations in Great Britain have set aside such blocks of airtime for South Asian, and, to a lesser extent, Afro-Caribbean programming.

Again, there are advantages and disadvantages. A great advantage is that the program is clearly identifiable as "ours" (the group's), and it can be scheduled regularly, so its appearance will be predictable. If it is produced at the mainstream station, and with the station's facilities and crew, its costs will be far lower than if the group attempted a production of roughly the same quality on its own. But if

23

the mainstream staff feels no particular obligation to work with minority groups, that advantage disappears. The predictability of scheduling also can mean the disadvantage of making it easy for hostile or disinterested audiences to avoid the program entirely.

*Separate stations* for ethnic minorities have been touted as the best solution to the problems of minority stereotyping and underrepresentation in some countries. New Zealand (Maori), Canada (Native Americans and some Asian émigré populations), Australia (Aborigines, some Asian émigré populations), the United States (Native Americans), the Scandinavian nations (Sami, or "Lapp,"), and Great Britain (Caribbean, South Asian), as well as some Third World nations (e.g., Ecuador, Nicaragua, Chile, Peru, Brazil, for Amerindians), have licensed such operations at one time or another.

Such stations have some very clear advantages. The groups involved with them enjoy something close to full control over their own portrayals (although not all members of a given minority group may agree with those portrayals). There is relatively unrestricted access to program time, depending upon the size of the budget. (Talent may be in short supply at first, but generally becomes more plentiful as stations establish themselves, particularly as outlets for ethnic minority pop music.) Scheduling can be done as the group thinks best. If the groups also aim to reach the majority culture audience at least some of the time, that larger public knows exactly where to find their broadcasts. And there is high symbolic value to a group's having its own station; it is a mark of the group's modernity and importance, especially if broadcast facilities throughout the country are in short supply.

Some disadvantages are quite obvious. Costs of running such stations are considerable: Even volunteer-staffed community radio stations in the United States usually have annual budgets above U.S. $200,000. Ethnic minority television stations are extremely rare, mainly because of the prohibitive costs associated with TV. Majority culture audiences find it easy to avoid listening to such stations, and mainstream stations can claim that they do not need to cover ethnic minority affairs, since the minorities can do that for themselves. If on-air staff members are inexperienced, as is often the case, minority and mainstream audiences alike may criticize minority station programs for their lack of (mainstream) "professionalism." Older ethnic minority listeners often have little tolerance for mispronunciations or misusage of ethnic minority languages by young announcers, many of whom have very limited command of those languages. Also, thanks to their symbolic value and physical prominence, ethnic minority stations may risk becoming pawns in power struggles within minority groups, as happened in certain Canadian Mohawk stations during the so-called Oka crisis of 1990.

There are approaches which fall short of ownership or administration of an ethnic minority station, but which still allow for control of broadcast content at regularly scheduled airtimes. Norway, Sweden, and Denmark all operate *närradio* ("near radio," but "community radio" might be a better descriptive translation) services, to which groups (but not individuals) of virtually every imaginable sort may apply for time to broadcast over government-furnished and -financed transmitters. If increasing numbers of groups apply to use *närradio,* the authorities attempt to increase the numbers of transmitters; in Stockholm, where demand is particularly heavy, there are now four transmitters dedicated to *närradio.* Groups must agree to broadcast at least once a week, for a minimum of 15 minutes, throughout the entire year. This is meant to ensure that groups will be serious about the undertaking, but also that they will not indulge in "hit and run" broadcasting, with sudden and harsh attacks on others, perhaps followed by an equally sudden disappearance from the airwaves.

Attacks do occur. An Islamic fundamentalist spokesperson living in Stockholm and broadcasting through *närradio* there made some vicious attacks on Jews and on other Islamic groups during spring 1993. The *närradio* licensing authorities in each country may remove groups from the air for offenses such as incitement to riot. However, legally enforceable definitions of offenses often are lacking; in the case of the Islamic fundamentalist, he remains on the air, despite attempts by Sweden's *närradiokomiten* to remove him. He claims, with some justification, that Sweden's freedom of speech laws protect him. In fact, all three countries try to encourage the maximum degree of freedom of speech through *närradio,* and would much rather negotiate a settlement with a group than take it off the air.

Groups using *närradio*—hundreds of them, ranging from religious organizations to student associations (the Jewish Students' Association at the University of Stockholm offers one 15-minute program per week)—must supply their own studio equipment and talent, as well as the link between the studio and the *närradio* transmitter. The former usually can be managed at low cost, and talent usually consists of unpaid volunteers; the latter is subsidized by the government. Ethnic minorities are not major users of the facilities, but many South European, North African, and Middle Eastern "guest workers," students, and others are active in the larger cities: Oslo, Stockholm, Gothenburg, Copenhagen. They may broadcast in their own languages (which sometimes makes it difficult for the authorities to monitor them), the majority culture language(s), or a mixture of the two.

A few nations, such as Great Britain, South Africa, and New Zealand, have developed more modest forms of *närradio.* Groups may seek authorization to broadcast locally for a limited period of time (often for folk festivals, local fairs, school events, etc.) with no promise of renewal, over broadcast frequencies more (New Zealand) or less (South Africa, Great Britain) reserved for the purpose. However, the groups themselves must cover virtually all costs of operation; only the actual transmission is covered by the government. Despite that financial handicap, and the uncertain prospects of longer-term licensing, many groups have taken advantage of the opportunity, including Caribbean and South Asian associations in Great Britain, and Maori and other South Pacific islanders in New Zealand. They see temporary authorization as a way to gain experience and to publicize themselves. Most of the roughly two dozen Maori stations in New Zealand began life as temporary services, as did a number of the South Asian and Caribbean stations now holding full time licenses in Great Britain. (However, more of the latter got their "battle scars" through illegal transmissions, and some of them were forced off the airwaves four, five, or more times.)

Cable television has led to yet another form of potential involvement for ethnic minorities: "access" channels. Such channels, which exist in the United States, Canada, and several European nations, are set aside for the use of community groups, who usually enjoy considerable freedom of speech through them. The cable operators, the local governments, or various combinations of the two finance offices which offer help with production and editing for users. When their productions are ready for broadcast, the cable operations usually publicize them. Access channels are a useful way for ethnic minority groups to gain experience with TV, and many have taken advantage of the opportunity, which usually costs them nothing but their own labors.

However, they have two major disadvantages. First, rarely is there any guarantee of regularly scheduled airtime, provided that groups would want it. That limits the ability of most groups to develop loyal audiences. Second, many present-day cable operations feature 30, 40, or more channels. With so many choices, and with limited publicity for any one group's access channel program, most viewers probably will remain unaware of access programming. If they are aware, they may regard it as "unprofessional," which it usually is by the standards of the broadcast industry. Some viewers then may watch it only to see the "amusing" mistakes and other lapses in "professionalism" that many access programs exhibit. Others may watch for content, and forgive such "deficiencies."

\* \* \* \* \*

As some of the advantages associated with certain approaches become the disadvantages of still others, it clearly seems best for ethnic minority groups to be covered by and to work through all types of channels. Coverage of minorities through mainstream channels helps to ensure that larger, and perhaps more diverse, majority culture audiences will see and hear them. That should lessen the likelihood they will consider themselves, or be considered

*Separate and Mainstream Broadcasting*

by others, as removed from national life. News coverage is especially important in that regard: It is much more difficult for anyone consciously or unconsciously wishing to avoid exposure to their viewpoints to do so when items about them are included in the overall news programs.

> *For these reasons, the Commission on Radio and Television Policy observed that "A small portion of separated programming is insufficient," and recommended that "large-audience channels and their most-watched news and public affairs programs must include within their responsibilities adequate coverage of issues relating to minorities among the viewers."*

The use of separate channels undoubtably has advantages, but, where TV is concerned, it is likely to be some time before separate stations for ethnic minorities become available. "Närtelevision" services would be a possible intermediate step, if governments were willing to support the costs of transmission; many groups probably could afford the increasingly low-cost cameras, switching units, and recorders that would be needed. But *närradio* services were developed at the end of the 1970s, when world economies (including Scandinavian) were more robust than they are at present, so that finding money to support *närtelevision* might prove difficult. The present economic slump seems to have contributed to increasing manifestations of "anti-foreigner" bias there and in much of the rest of the industrialized world; that bias sometimes has included ethnic minorities in general, foreign or not. That is a strong argument for increasing the visibility of ethnic minorities, but it also may mean that there will be a great deal of opposition to government financing or any other form of state support for such services.

29

Despite the additional cost and other drawbacks, the very existence of minority-owned and -operated stations, and, to a more limited extent, *närradio,* tells minorities that they count for something in society as a whole. They also help to provide a sense of community, to lead to a renewed feeling of cultural pride, and to bring majority culture audiences to realize that there is much that different cultures can learn from one another. They may even bring mainstream broadcasters to realize that there is more than one valid approach to broadcasting!

Still, such exposures are not sufficient, if only because of their brevity, lack of widespread availability, and the ease with which majority culture audiences may avoid them. Therefore, mainstream broadcasts of longer interviews, discussions, and documentaries portraying minority viewpoints also are essential. If those programs can feature popular and respected (by majority and minorities alike) hosts, that should improve chances of reaching majority culture viewers. In any case, it is essential that station staff make every attempt to assist minority culture interviewees to tell their own stories, but in ways that the majority audience will understand. Staff members should act as bridges between their guests and viewers, which does *not* mean that they should be uncritical.

> *Both the large-audience channels as well as the minority channels can benefit from insights brought to bear by minority journalists.*
> *The Commission recommended that "to foster the understanding of minorities by majority audiences, minorities should be encouraged to make programming about their own culture for the majority audience and in the language of the majority."*

# COVERAGE OF CONFLICT
# AND ETHNIC MINORITIES

Decisions as to whether and how to cover conflicts in general, but those involving ethnic minorities in particular, can be terribly divisive. Is it better to ignore conflict in the interest of not overexciting the larger population? Or is it better to address conflict whenever and wherever it occurs, so that the public will know that the media aren't hiding anything, and can be trusted to cover conflict fairly?

On closer examination, four approaches seem to emerge. The first hopes that if conflict is *not* covered, perhaps it will diminish or disappear. During her tenure in office, British Prime Minister Margaret Thatcher often spoke of the need to deprive the Irish Republican Army of "the oxygen of publicity." By that, she meant that IRA spokespersons should be kept off the air; if the IRA's bombings, kidnappings, and other overt acts of "terrorism" absolutely had to be covered, at least IRA officials shouldn't be allowed to justify them.

But Prime Minister Thatcher's approach did acknowledge that some forms of conflict had to be portrayed. The actual coverage of IRA acts by the British media would illustrate a second approach to dealing with conflict: Portray that conflict so that public opinion can be mobilized in opposition to one of the parties involved. That in turn might help the party in the "right" to bring an end to the conflict more swiftly, since it could increase public tolerance of higher costs and greater limits on individual liberty in the interest of longer-term security.

Of course, such an approach does nothing to address underlying causes of the conflict. A third approach would portray two (or more) sides in a conflict, but do so in such a way that one party, whether the current government, business, a union, the military, or whoever else holds most power, will be portrayed as most "right" of all, or at least more "right" than any other party. If there can be presentation of possible concessions or adjustments, that may be helpful. Meaningful adjustments should help to address the root causes of the conflict, while less than meaningful ones may serve to satisfy the majority that at least there's some willingness to negotiate.

A fourth approach involves making a major effort to convey to audiences a clear and balanced (or at least multifaceted) picture of the conflict: its origins, its nature, and possible paths to its resolution. Although this fourth approach may seem easily most logical of all, it is likely to be the most difficult to implement. Governments or other holders of power may strongly resist media attempts to furnish anything other than a completely or heavily one-sided portrayal of conflict, perhaps because they truly believe that there *is* only one valid side. The more autonomous the media are, the better their chances become of prevailing in the face of government opposition.

However, opposition may come from other quarters. The majority culture in general can find it very reassuring to share the belief in one point of view. U.S. commercial television networks received much criticism during the late 1950s and early 1960s for their relatively balanced coverage of the civil rights movement; government officials and law enforcement agencies, but also members of the general public, questioned the wisdom and the propriety of showing violators of the law in a favorable light. Those living in southern states (but elsewhere, as well) also were quite likely to express the fear that authority in general, or at least what they regarded as *legitimate* authority, would be eroded through such broadcasts. Great Britain, New Zealand, and other western nations with sizable and active ethnic minority populations have seen similar outbursts of criticism following television's coverage of major demonstrations or confrontations involving those minorities. And Japanese society seems uncomfortable with the media revelation of conflict per se.

All four of those approaches may be in use during the same period of time, depending upon the nature of the conflict. Even highly repressive governments sometimes find it useful to allow the media relatively free rein in the coverage of one or another form of conflict, so long as it does not seem to challenge the existing order in any fundamental way; that can help to increase media credibility. Since there is no single "correct" way to cover all forms of conflict, broadcasters will take different approaches.

Still, one cannot ignore the very real problems often faced by conflict-ridden societies, where *any* approach is bound to lead to problems. Nor is it surprising to discover attempts to ignore or to provide highly biased coverage of certain sides in certain conflicts—or for there to be criticism of the media when they *do* try to provide relatively balanced coverage of them, because of the almost inevitable differences of opinion within society concerning conflict and its coverage. Conflict involving ethnic minorities often displays even sharper differences of opinion, since ethnic minorities have had long experience with media neglect or distortion of their viewpoints; majorities, for their part, often are unaccustomed to seeing and hearing, much less acknowledging, minority viewpoints, and may resent or reject them almost automatically.

It may be tempting to conclude that the media cannot possibly satisfy everyone, and perhaps should limit themselves to satisfying the majority culture. However, consider for a moment the increasing availability of audio- and videocassette technology, fax, e-mail, and many other channels that can be used for something approaching mass communication. Many of those technologies also have undergone a physical transformation from once bulky (therefore, easy to detect) pieces of equipment into small, highly portable (therefore, easy to conceal) gear. They have rendered it almost impossible for most governments or other power-holders to place a *cordon sanitaire* around the populace at large, or prevent or discourage the circulation of minority viewpoints. Increasingly, much of the population *will* have access to alternative points of view, which is quite likely to mean that they will distrust mainstream media all the more when those media ignore or distort conflict.

A vivid example of the ways in which electronic technology has altered the ability of governments to control the flow of information within national borders, as well as beyond them, is the Tiananmen Square incident in Beijing in 1989. In earlier years, the government of the People's Republic of China would have had little difficulty in surrounding the largely student-led "prodemocracy" demonstrations with a near-total news blackout. Even after correspondents from the United States, Great Britain, and other Western nations were allowed to report from the PRC, there were limits on what could be reported, and means of enforcing those limits.

However, by June of 1989, certain Chinese students had access to facsimile machines. Correspondents covering their activities could report directly on them by relaying material directly to their home countries through communication satellites. Reports from those countries then would came back into China through the Voice of America, BBC World Services, and other international radio stations, as well as through fax messages from Chinese students abroad to their compatriots back home. Some of the fax messages themselves became elements in VOA, BBC, and other reports to China. Videocassette cameras, sometimes operated by the students themselves, recorded startling images of the conflict; a number of those cassettes, small enough to conceal in various ways, brought those images onto TV screens in many parts of the world. There were too many alternative channels of communication available for the authorities to be able to block them all.

There is yet another reason for countries faced with internal conflict involving ethnic minorities to make genuine efforts to cover it, and to do so with some degree of balance. If a group opposed to the government is successful in getting its point of view through to domestic and international audiences, despite attempts of authorities to ignore it or to present it in one-sided fashion, then there is a strong likelihood that such success will encourage the opposition to feel that victory cannot be far off, now that it has a place on the world stage. It may even make the opposition more intransigent, and add to the severity of the conflict. Something of the sort appears to have occurred in Afghanistan, where various opposition groups, often representing different ethnic groups, managed to gain coverage through western news media. That appears in turn to have encouraged them to feel that western coverage would mean western support, moral and monetary, for each of their particular viewpoints or causes. That perception cannot have made it any easier for the various groups to negotiate a compromise among themselves when the Communist government finally fell.

35

*In spite of these very real dilemmas, a policy of not covering conflicts will do little to solve the problems and, as President Jimmy Carter commented, "Especially in times of crisis, citizens need to know the truth." The Commission of Radio and Television Policy agreed that "television stations should not avoid serious coverage of ethnic conflict in the mistaken belief that such coverage worsens the situation. In fact, failure to explain a controversial issue fosters the ignorance and misunderstanding that may be the cause of the tension in the first place." When rumor and hearsay take over, the "effects are likely to be far more dangerous."*

***When to initiate coverage of conflict:*** One often hears that a given conflict has taken a country by surprise. Doubtless that is true for a limited number of situations where groups, and not individuals who have highly specific grudges and causes, are concerned. (Individuals often do seem to arise from nowhere, although their actions *may* be more predictable if one accepts the notion that media coverage of a certain form of conflict sometimes inspires others to imitate it.) In most cases, however, careful consideration will reveal that a group, whether ethnic minority or majority, placing itself in conflict with mainstream or minority society, had been displaying various early warning signals of an intent to act.

But would earlier, more complete, more balanced coverage of the grievances of such groups necessarily help to avert or resolve ultimate conflict? Almost certainly not if a group is bent on confrontation. Such groups rarely see much hope of resolution, at least in any terms that the larger society would find acceptable. Early disclosure might prevent a group from taking a particular action at a particular time, but it is doubtful that the group could be dissuaded from making a similar attempt elsewhere, even with more balanced media coverage of the reasons for its opposition to society.

There are many other facets of the difficulty of providing early coverage of potential conflict. For one thing, is there the risk that early media coverage of a group's point of view, as expressed in words or deeds, will unduly alarm the larger society, especially if the means at a group's disposal appear to limit its ability to carry out its threat? Or might such early warning give society the time needed to resolve disagreements and thus head off larger, more costly conflicts? For another, might early coverage of a group's disagreements with the larger society actually inspire the group to consider escalation of conflict, now that it had the attention of the media? And for a third, how does the choice of spokespersons, whether made by the media themselves or for the media by others, affect media portrayal of the conflict? If made by the media, will there be a tendency to emphasize sensational or unusual elements? And will this be done at the expense of information that would help the public to understand why such a group might develop in the first place, and how likely it might be to enter into direct conflict with the larger society? If made for the media by others, how true a picture will society receive of the group's aims? Spokespersons often are chosen by groups because they will come across well in print or on TV as rational, deliberative, and even conciliatory, when the group's chief decision-makers may be quite the opposite.

There are no perfectly correct or comprehensive answers to any of those questions, if only because we can never know with certainty where an alternative course of action through choice of a different form of media coverage at a different moment might have led. But media personnel do need to be aware of any early warning signs that may indicate incipient conflict: leaflets, wall posters, graffiti, popular music, rallies, and other manifestations all may provide hints of what might come. Many of those signs will be nothing more than symbols of momentary or personal discontent; some will be juvenile pranks. Knowing how to discern the difference between serious, casual, or false signs comes only with time and experience. Ethnic minorities often develop symbolic languages of their own, particularly when they do not speak something other than the majority culture language. African-American rap (hip-hop) music is full of redefined majority culture terminology, as well as slang based upon it. Nonverbal behavior, particularly gestures, may be very different for minority cultures than it is for majority cultures. All of that would seem ample reason for a media organization to leave reporters in place once they acquire some expertise with respect to a group, and to provide them with the time and support necessary to follow developing stories of conflict once it appears. The *Washington Post's* support of its Watergate reporters, Woodward and Bernstein, was exemplary, and also was an excellent example of media autonomy from the government. However, it was not common in 1973, and seems even less so now.

*Long-term strategies:* Early coverage of conflict and ethnic minorities involves adopting a long-term strategy in dealing with it, although it is always possible that those early signs will turn out to have been false alarms. On balance, however, provision of early coverage does appear to be wise, and false alarms will be few, if skilled reporters with experience in covering conflict are assigned to such stories. Lacking early coverage, one of two things is likely to happen: Either most or all conflicts will be treated as serious issues, which may lead the public to take none of them seriously (recall the legend of the shepherd boy who cried "wolf!" far too often); or few or none will be treated seriously, at least by the mainstream media, which may lead the public to look elsewhere (clandestine media, foreign broadcasts) for more information about a conflict which they have learned of through gossip and rumor.

Perhaps the most important thing for experienced reporters and media administrators alike to bear in mind when preparing long-term strategies for coverage of conflict of any sort, but especially if it involves ethnic minorities, is the need to avoid the sort of stereotyped consideration of minorities and conflict that can arise after years of covering it and of seeing, hearing, and reading coverage of it by others. There can be temptations to stereotype through concentration on sensational elements, just as there can be temptations to emphasize the differences between minority and majority aspirations, ignoring such similarities as may exist.

*Avoid Stereotyping*

*In general, whether in stories about conflicts or other, more routine events, it is important, as the Commission recommended, to "avoid stereotyping of minority groups and individuals. Cover minorities in interaction with other groups. Do not always link certain ethnic groups to particular stories."*

There also is the cynicism that treats all conflict as if it were inevitable, but, in the final analysis, forgettable: Today's conflict lasts only until another arises to take its place, and furnishes fresh footage of violence, oddity, or anger. Anyone who has visited or worked in newsrooms probably recalls at least a few instances when a news editor has said something along the lines of, "Well, let's drop that item (on conflict) now. We've used it in three newscasts over the past 12 hours." Granted, news items die sooner or later, but items involving conflict, especially when linked to ethnic minorities, would seem to deserve consideration for prolonged carriage on more than strictly quantitative grounds.

There are two other considerations regarding long-term strategies for the coverage of conflict. The first involves development of a thorough, constantly updated archival collection of items about conflict, and especially about the groups and individuals, minority and majority cultures alike, espousing it. It also should contain information about groups and individuals who can provide expert assessment of such activities. If systematically organized, the collection will provide a near-continuous gauge of activity, but it also will provide a sense of context and history—two elements that often are lacking in media coverage of conflict. If it is cross-indexed, reporters and commentators seeking information on specific groups or individuals could look for them under their own names, but also under categories of activity, employment, etc. Staff effort required to maintain such an archive is considerable, but it often pays handsome dividends in bringing patterns of activity out of what probably would have appeared to be isolated incidents. A good archive also permits sounder speculation about the future course of events, since it provides a more comprehensive picture of past activity.

Ideally, archives will be readily and easily accessible to reporters, editors, and managers. Computer files are preferable, but the costs of staffing necessary to keep them updated may be prohibitive. (However, reporters and others should be familiar with such relevant computerized data bases as already exist.) The time-honored method of clipping and filing bits of hard copy can serve perfectly well. Archivists themselves must become familiar with the practices of media staff, so as to determine the most helpful and readily accessible ways to record and organize material.

The same point applies with equal force to a station's development and maintenance of a list of spokespersons and experts on conflict, ethnic minority affairs, and other subjects. Reporters and editors often have a tendency to turn to the same limited list of spokespersons and experts time after time, in part because that eliminates the need to search for new sources. Ireland's Radio Telefis Eirann developed a list of female experts on a variety of topics, including conflict and ethnic minority affairs, complete with telephone and fax numbers, addresses, brief descriptions of expertise, etc. It was organized by subject matter, making it easy for reporters to locate appropriate individuals. Not all reporters use it, but those who do have found it useful in enlarging the variety of opinions and viewpoints presented in their stories.

The second consideration applies particularly to conflicts involving ethnic minorities. A culturally homogeneous news department may be able to cover such conflicts, but its staff is almost certain to miss some very important facets of them. There are many good reasons for employing ethnic minorities as reporters, editors, and managers—for one thing, they can supply fresh perspectives on coverage of *majority* cultures—but one major reason is that they are more likely to pick up those facets of minority culture experience and perception that may be missed by majority culture staff. That isn't inevitable: minorities in the newsroom can be "ghettoized" by their majority culture colleagues, and thus play little active role in news gathering. They also may be underutilized for their special skills and insights, as appeared to have happened for many years in the newsroom of the New Zealand Broadcasting Corporation. Maori staff were treated by most of their *pakeha* (white) colleagues as if they were "brown pakeha," and thus shared the basic assumptions of the majority culture. Few white reporters or editors requested the insights they could have provided on Maori affairs, which often were covered by whites. The point is not that it was inappropriate for whites to provide such coverage, or that only Maori were qualified to provide it; rather, a fusion of their efforts could lead to more balanced and accurate reporting, and to a better understanding of how to communicate effectively with majority and minority culture listeners alike.

There is one further caveat regarding minority culture staff. It is quite possible that certain individuals from minority cultures have lost touch with, or even rejected, their cultural roots, in which case their insights will differ little from those of their majority culture colleagues. A Maori or Aborigine or Native American who attends largely white boarding schools and colleges, serves in the largely white military, and then becomes a journalist, may have very little sense of, or respect for, her or his original culture. Thus, her or his "insights" probably will be no more (or less) valid than those of any majority culture journalist. That is all the more likely when there are few, if any, fellow minorities on staff.

However, one should always be aware of the possibility that, when interethnic conflict erupts, even reporters with seemingly long-forgotten ethnic or tribal roots may recover their sense of identity, or may find themselves the targets of attempts at influence applied by members of their groups. That does not invalidate their contributions, but it may call for some measure of vigilance on the part of supervisors and colleagues. Any advice given by the latter regarding indications that ethnic minority staff are letting their biases show will be far more effective if those supervisors and colleagues have managed to keep their own biases under control.

***Short-term strategies:*** There will be those occasions when a conflict arises so swiftly and unpredictably that the media must employ short-term strategies. Many of the points made about long-term strategies apply with equal force here: Well-kept archives will be helpful, as will the knowledge of experienced majority and minority culture staff. If the event turns out to be something completely new (usually it does not), there will be many more questions than answers at first. The clearest, most concise answers (which of course are ideal, given limited airtime) will also seem the most compelling. Reporters should be wary of them: If the conflict really is that sudden and unpredictable, such answers should not be plentiful. It would be more prudent to indicate in initial reports that much remains unknown for the moment.

Still, nature abhors a vacuum, and, presuming the conflict continues, a station or network will have to be prepared to devote time to finding answers. A few newsrooms have developed full-time crisis investigation teams, made up of individuals whose characters and backgrounds lend themselves to rapid but thorough investigation. They are skilled in assembling material, detecting crucial gaps in a story and in the responses of key individuals connected with it, and in maintaining calmness in the face of uncertainty and even panic. Smaller newsrooms may have one or two individuals, rather than entire teams, who are especially apt for such work, but editors must be prepared to release them from their usual duties at a moment's notice. Large national broadcast organizations may be in a better position to develop and maintain such teams.

During its early years, CNN used an unofficial E-Team (for Emergency) to handle fast-breaking crises. The idea of the E-Team was based on the notion that the most senior or skilled professionals are not always available when crises erupt. However, if all of the experience and quick-response capability of the station could be pooled and *always* be available, then the dangers of incomplete or inaccurate coverage would be significantly reduced. In the CNN model, the senior producers, staff coordinators, writers, and technical personnel were expected to be always on call. In a crisis, no matter when it occurred, the E-Team was summoned and immediately responsive.

Even without the luxury of such teams, some very small stations have been able to respond quickly and resourcefully to crises. Radio station WOBJ-FM in Hayward, Wisconsin, is licensed to the Lac Court Oreilles band of the Objibwa nation (Native American). When the state of Wisconsin guaranteed Ojibwa rights to spearfishing in certain northern Wisconsin lakes, and the Ojibwa sought to exercise those rights, they met with strong and violent opposition from some white fishermen, resort owners, and others. The station broadcast a number of special news reports and discussion programs on the confrontation, being careful to cover a wide range of viewpoints. It was able to do so in part because station staff had a wide range of acquaintances, and could identify appropriate individuals quickly. It is

44

impossible to know whether the broadcasts themselves helped to reduce tension, but they certainly provided a picture of the various points of view, and the reasons underlying them, that was considerably broader and more detailed than what was available through mainstream media.

Journalists sometimes have pooled their experiences with the coverage of conflict and ethnic minorities, and have produced guidelines on the "dos and don'ts" of journalistic conduct, especially in unanticipated, fast-breaking situations. The U.S. Radio-Television News Directors Association, a professional organization, developed such a set of guidelines following the outbreak of disturbances in various inner-city settings (Watts-Los Angeles, Detroit, Newark) in the mid- to late 1960s. The guidelines were advisory, and stemmed from the actual experiences of reporters who had covered such events, but also of editors who had to make quick decisions as to whether to broadcast certain reports or not, in what form, with what amount of editing, and for how long. For example, reporters were cautioned to make themselves as inconspicuous as possible when covering a demonstration, so that their very presence would not stimulate demonstrators to "act up" for the camera, perhaps improving prospects for actual broadcast of the event. There also were warnings about "false" spokespersons, who presented themselves quite convincingly as being at the very center of the action, when in fact they were bit players or even completely unconnected with the real leaders.

It is almost impossible to assess the usefulness of those guidelines, but subsequent television coverage of similar demonstrations and disturbances, e.g., the Los Angeles "riots" of April 1992 following the initial verdict on the police beating of Rodney King, seem to show greater caution on the part of journalists, especially in terms of oversensationalizing. There were some indications that transmission of the beating of a white truck driver by African-

Americans at the corner of Florence and Normandy Streets in the obvious absence of law enforcement officials, led others to seek to imitate that action. However, that coverage also appeared to prompt interventions by African-Americans to stop such beatings.

The increased miniaturization and portability of cameras and other equipment has helped reporters to make themselves less noticeable when they cover conflict. But the increased availability of direct transmission from the scene of the action to the TV studio, and then on to viewers, has made it far more difficult for editors to sit back and ponder the best approaches to covering such events, which they could do when the material had to be brought back to the studio, processed, edited, and then integrated with a newscast or special feature. There is something very compelling about being able to see a broadcast of an event as it occurs in "real time." TV coverage of conflict, perhaps especially of ethnic minorities involved in already tense situations such as Los Angeles in April 1992, calls for at least brief editorial deliberation of accuracy and context before it is broadcast, competitive pressures to be first on the air notwithstanding.

*The place of commentaries:* In both short- and long-term strategies for the coverage of conflict and ethnic minorities, news reporting probably will command primary attention, since there is a perceived need on the part of journalists and the public alike to have a readily available source of current information on local, national, and international developments. The sheer quantity of information can become overwhelming. It also can be confusing if bits and pieces of a given story become available at different times, making it difficult for the public to assemble a reasonably coherent image. The 1993 World Trade Center bombing in New York City is a good illustration:

Reports came rapidly, but it was difficult to find much sense of shape or coherence in them for some time.

Many stations seek to overcome that problem by furnishing backgrounders and commentaries. (In some nations, the term "commentary" covers background reports as well. We distinguish between them here.) Both are potentially valuable, but they proceed from quite different assumptions.

*Backgrounders* usually are based upon summaries of the major elements of a story; they are intended both to remind audiences of the facts and to draw conclusions from those facts which might help audiences to see the issues more clearly. A journalist's opinion should be absent or minimal; these are *not* editorials. However, it will be helpful to the audience if backgrounders can indicate something about the sources used to prepare them. It also would be helpful if there were some indication of gaps remaining in the story—an admission, in a way, of what the broadcaster still does not know, but will try to discover because it's important. Careful listeners and viewers may have an idea by the end of a backgrounder as to the station's attitude or feeling about the situation under examination; they also should have an idea of each side's positions, and actions in support of those positions, that does not stem from apparent bias on the station's part.

*Commentaries* may present summaries of facts, as well, but ordinarily will offer critical assessments along the lines of whether a given action was wise, a given inaction cowardly, etc. Some of the interpretation and opinion that forms those assessments may come from officials, experts, opinion leaders, etc., but the station is quite likely to add some of its own, particularly if certain of its staff have had considerable experience in covering a certain event, individual or group.

Commentaries certainly have a valid place in a broadcast schedule. Many commentators are highly skilled at giving shape to seemingly disparate elements of a story, but equally skilled, thanks to their often extensive experience as reporters, observers, or participants, at bringing critical perspectives to bear on it. If the central goal of a station is to lead all or most of the public, minorities and majorities alike, to believe its account of a situation, then anything involving opinions (those of the stations, but also those of the spokespersons they select) should be used with caution. It is quite easy for a station to assume that it is being "balanced" in its treatment of a situation involving conflict, but audiences listening and viewing in the heat of the moment can have very different impressions, perhaps because of a commentator's opinion which would be considered non-controversial in most circumstances. Conflict involving ethnic minorities has a way of increasing people's sensitivities, and opinions can act as lightning rods for them, particularly as the opposing sides first clash openly. Certainly opinions are essential when covering conflict. But do stations and networks necessarily serve their audiences well by seeming to endorse certain opinions, particularly their own?

There is a viable alternative. The BBC, and several other broadcasters, have had a long-standing practice of inviting outsiders to prepare and present commentaries. The outsiders may or may not be citizens of the broadcasting nation. They are selected because they will present differing viewpoints on given issues, and their credentials are an-nounced in such a way that audiences will have some perspective on their observations. The broadcaster usually indicates that it does not necessarily endorse the views presented. Perhaps the most difficult element in that approach is the selection of commentators who are more or less equally adept at presenting their points of view, and will present them in such a way that the audience isn't left feeling that there are few points of comparison, or that one of the commentators has been given advantages not available to the others (including larger blocks of air time, perhaps at better times of day).

The process of selecting commentators itself is very time-consuming. Stations should not consider furnishing commentaries unless they are willing to devote the requisite time to them. BBC-transmitted commentaries on ethnic minority confrontations with law enforcement officials in Brixton, Bristol, and many other cities in Great Britain were furnished by academic experts on law enforcement and ethnic minorities, law enforcement officials, public housing officials, religious and community leaders, government officials, and others. BBC staff relied on more than their own judgment and past experiences in compiling such a varied assortment: They also spoke with members of ethnic minority communities, law enforcement officials, etc., to learn whom *they* trusted, relied upon, turned to, for guidance in such situations.

Once appropriate commentators are found, they may be inept at presenting their views over radio or television. If so, broadcasters should be prepared to work with them, so that their presentations will not suffer greatly in comparison with those of other speakers. The U.S. Federal Communications Commission (FCC) developed a Fairness Doctrine in 1949. It was intended to help individuals and groups present points of view that were at variance with those expressed by or through radio and TV stations. One of its stipulations was that broadcasters should help presenters who lacked "professional" skills, so that they would at least begin to approach the level of a station's presenters. Even though the FCC did away with the Doctrine in 1987, some U.S. broadcasters still provide such assistance.

It also helps stations to maintain credibility if commentaries are clearly separated from other program elements. Clear aural and visual identification of them as commentaries, both at the beginning and at the end of the segment, is essential. If on television, commentaries can be differentiated from newscasts by placing commen-tators in clearly separated locations. The introduction of unusual aural and visual production techniques—filter microphones, unchanging chest shots throughout the commentary—could underline that differentiation, but they might prove so distracting or boring that they would interfere with the message.

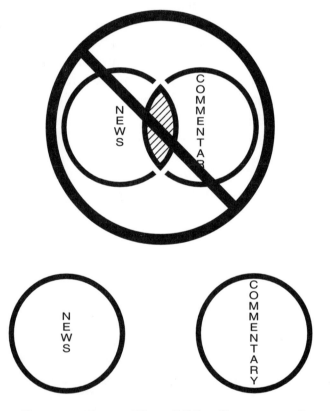

*Commentary Should be Separated*
*from News and Properly Identified*

In the final analysis, a station will want to ensure that use of a backgrounder or commentary in a given conflict situation truly helps the audience to better understand what is occurring within and between the opposing forces— not just one, but both (or all three or four) of them. If it does not, it seems of dubious value.

> *Whichever method of expanding news analysis is used, the television or radio station has a heavy responsibility. The Commission on Radio and Television Policy recommended that "commentary should always be separated from news coverage and clearly labeled." The Commission also urged that stations "provide commentary only when it will help understanding. If the journalists are not sufficiently informed, professional, and independent of the government, such a commentary will be regarded as reflecting the position of the government. That, in turn, may undermine the credibility of the government and the journalist among viewers."*

***Preparing for coverage of conflict:*** A further point regarding strategic approaches to the coverage of conflict was raised by the Commission on Radio and Television Policy in its recommendation that *television and radio stations "identify problems before they become crises."*

> *Minority group members should have direct access and coverage should include documentaries and other programs in addition to news programs. Broadcasters should develop the capacity to foresee the possibility*

51

*of conflict, and then consider what they
might do to address its causes before
it actually breaks out.*

That is no easy matter, since the groups involved may not find it possible to articulate their grievances, or may adopt an attitude along the lines of, "You lack the capacity to understand us, so why should we attempt to explain ourselves to you?" They also may do everything possible to conceal their aims, so as to have the benefit of surprise, and perhaps the increased media attention that is likely to result. However, it certainly is worthwhile for the media to make the effort to discover what they can, as early as they can. In the process, if their aim appears to others to be a genuine understanding of a group's fundamental grievances, that itself may create a sufficient climate of trust to persuade the group to adopt a nonviolent approach.

What the Report really asks stations to do is to develop the sort of early warning system noted above. What it asks stations to reject is a quite common media attitude that conflicts are worth considering only when they've emerged publicly, and often begin to exhibit their more colorful, sensational characteristics, making for livelier television coverage.

It may be useful for stations to undertake a form of role-playing in which they set for themselves hypothetical exercises based on real-life conflict situations. An illustrative example:

Let's presume that we've just received an unconfirmed report that a number of street gangs in City X are meeting to determine whether they should pool their forces and seek a major confrontation with the police. How can we confirm this? If it's correct, what can we learn about why the groups are considering it? If any of their reasons seems valid, could the furnishing of media publicity at this time help to defuse the situation?

If, for whatever reason, it is not feasible to hold such mock fire-drills, stations should at the very least develop contingency plans for the coverage of conflicts of the sorts most likely to appear in their coverage area.

Development of an early-warning-and-response system should take into account one further element. Conflicts involving ethnic minorities often give rise to the expression of quite extreme viewpoints. Audiences should be aware of such viewpoints, but extremist views should not have the stage to themselves unless they truly seem that dominant. It sometimes is more difficult to search out the more moderate, often less colorful, viewpoint, especially if reporters wait until the eruption of conflict to attempt to discover it: By then, the moderate spokesperson often stands little chance of being heard, and may even not dare to express such a view, if "extremists" already have claimed the bulk of media attention and seem to command the support of their reference group. Comprehensive lists of resource persons and ethnic minority reporters, editors, and supervisors are particularly relevant here: They are the sources that will facilitate the discovery of those other voices.

However, media staff should always be aware that, in certain forms of conflict—particularly intraethnic, but also interethnic when groups live in "mixed" neighborhoods, as in Los Angeles, parts of Bosnia, or throughout Trinidad— it can be very risky for a moderate spokesperson to utter her or his views, especially to reporters for a broadcast service identified with the majority culture. That is especially true of television, where individuals can be identified visually and aurally. The use of electronic "masks" and voice distortion often is not enough to protect the individual's identity. Media staff should be particularly aware that, while "leading spokespersons" may be well aware of potential risks (which they probably dismiss; otherwise, they wouldn't have assumed such positions), individuals who aren't accustomed to being interviewed by the media probably are not as aware of them. The media sometimes do have the responsibility of protecting people from themselves (or their neighbors), and inexperienced interviewees should be given some idea of how their comments are likely to be used within a broadcast.

*Ensuring the safety of journalists:* It is the task of journalists themselves to be sensitive to the potential dangers to ordinary citizens of interviewing them and then displaying their voices and faces on television during conflicts. But there also are dangers for journalists in those and other conflict situations. Few years go by without at least a hundred imprisoned, and a few dozen dead or seriously injured, as a direct result of covering conflicts. Some of that is inevitable, in much the same way that fire department personnel, law enforcement officials, or construction workers on bridges and skyscrapers often are in hazardous situations in which some of them are killed. Some of those deaths are accidental, but law enforcement officials and journalists often find themselves in situations where someone may be quite ready to kill them. Unlike law enforcement officials, journalists usually are unarmed. Furthermore, seeking protection from law enforcement officials may be the last thing journalists would do in certain countries, where the government may wish to silence them, and often will do so through law enforcement agencies.

Journalists do have international associations, which sometimes are effective at bringing pressure to bear on governments to obtain the release of a colleague from detention. The World Press Freedom Committee, various of the Committees to Protect Journalists, the International Press Institute, International PEN, the International Committee of the Red Cross (which initiated a "hotline" service in 1985 to assist journalists going on hazardous missions), and others have been successful in obtaining the release of imprisoned journalists. Still, while there are no official figures available, the overall success rate of the organizations certainly is below 50 percent.

It would help if there were a truly universal protocol ensuring the protection of journalists, both domestically and internationally. Prospects for that appear slim, in light of the fact that many nations do not have extradition treaties with one another, and even those that do will not always observe them; thus, there is little likelihood that journalists will fare any better. But if a number of relatively powerful nations could reach such an agreement among themselves, they might be able to apply their collective weight to situations involving countries outside their ranks.

The UNESCO report *Many Voices, One World* (1980) raised the possibility of licensing journalists. Nations would determine whether individual journalists were qualified, in light of several criteria, to report on events taking place within their borders. Interethnic conflict is especially sensitive since, in many nations, political parties often form along ethnic lines, and parties in power are especially sensitive to the political impact of reporting on such conflict. For example, it was extremely difficult for reporters, domestic or foreign, to cover interethnic conflict in Zimbabwe in the mid-1980s, which involved the Shona people—the country's president, Robert Mugabe, is Shona—and the N'debele, the people of Mugabe's then-chief rival, Joshua Nkomo.

Under a licensing plan, licensed journalists would enjoy the protection of the government. However, it was and still is quite clear that any government wishing to withdraw that protection could do so immediately and without notice, on the grounds—sometimes justified—that a journalist had fabricated material or had broken the law. A government upset over an unflattering, but accurate, portrait of its handling of domestic ethnic minority conflict, as presented by a journalist, could just as easily claim that the law had been broken when it had not. Thus, licensing is not a viable solution.

\* \* \* \* \*

The coverage of conflict involving ethnic minorities is one of the most important functions of television. In part, that is because television is so widely viewed and so readily believed. Survey after survey in country after country indicates that citizens are willing to believe television's account of events over the accounts furnished by any other medium of mass communication. High viewing figures for TV's coverage of major conflicts involving ethnic minorities in recent years, whether on a national level (civil wars in Liberia, Sudan, and Bosnia, Hindu-Muslim clashes in India) or a local level (the Los Angeles "riots" of 1992, fighting in the Black townships surrounding Johannesburg), are a partial indication of television's primacy in that regard.

With that primacy should come a deep sense of responsibility to be fair, accurate, comprehensive, and balanced. Here, the record is uneven and inconsistent. Sometimes, that is not the fault of broadcast staff. If law enforcement, military, or government officials will not permit media access to certain battle sectors, documents, or important individuals, the most that broadcasters can do is to indicate that access was denied, as many of them did when the military placed narrow limits on their freedom of movement and of access to information during the Persian Gulf War, and as many do in attempting to report from Bosnia,

56

Liberia, India, Sri Lanka, and other current scenes of ethnic conflict. At the same time, the media must continue to seek access, preferably through accepted channels, but sometimes outside them *if* there is a genuine conviction on the part of media staff that it is truly the *public* (including majority and minority publics) interest that will be served first and foremost.

A few surveys have indicated that the public is skeptical of media claims that journalists should have access to certain situations and material connected with conflict, e.g., graphic visual evidence of beatings, torture, or other forms of intense physical abuse. Some of the public believe this coverage is sought chiefly, or only, because the sensational nature of the material will increase viewership. Some surveys also indicate that there is considerable public support for various restrictions on access to material connected with conflict, as is in fact often the case with major wars (the Gulf War, certainly), but also with more modest forms of conflict (raids on alleged drug dealers, who often are members of ethnic minority groups, by U.S. narcotics squads; the breaking up by South African police of anti-apartheid, anti-Inkatha, or anti-African National Congress demonstrations). Public support for restricting the media may arise because the media sometimes are perceived as "out for themselves" and unwilling to cooperate with governments and their agencies to help maintain the status quo.

The public may feel that way because some regard the media as one-dimensional in their approach to the coverage of violence, seeking out what is colorful, vivid, startling, and, above all, action-filled. By that token, conflict is useful to the media because it *moves*. When it ceases to do so, it quickly loses its place in the news lineup, even though the negotiations that may follow it show promise of success. Unfortunately, negotiations rarely produce physical action, nor are they visually compelling in most other respects. Certain critics contend that if broadcasters want to see an end to a conflict, it is because the public is likely to grow tired of watching it fairly soon, anyway. Those broadcasters who choose to present coverage of the less intensely visual aspects of conflict, they claim, will do so late at night, or on Sunday morning, when the viewing audience is quite modest no matter what is being broadcast.

There are many examples of news reports and programs that refute those conclusions. A fair share of them come from public broadcasting stations, such as several probing and lengthy discussions in 1992 and 1993 of German violence against Turks, Vietnamese, and other émigrés and guest workers living in Germany, televised by the two German public services, ARD and ZDF, during prime time. Commercial services have followed such practices, as well, as certain TV stations in Los Angeles did during the "riots" of 1992, or as Granada Television of Great Britain did in 1988 when it prepared a prime-time documentary ("Death on the Rock") on the killing of two suspected IRA terrorists by British police in Gibraltar. All of those situations were rich in vivid visual elements, but the programs themselves were devoted largely to a careful, although hardly dispassionate, consideration of the history, implications, and other relatively nonvisual dimensions of the events. "Talking heads" were plentiful. Audiences were sizable.

Are public perceptions of television's "preoccupation" with action inaccurate? Probably not, although the public may exaggerate the degree of preoccupation. Television is a visual medium, but "visual," as just noted, is generally interpreted by broadcasters as something that moves—and "talking heads" engaged in deep discussion, or newscasters reading copy from a teleprompter, don't display much movement. Furthermore, drama and situation comedy— often based loosely or closely on contemporary life—feature a great deal of movement. There is a tendency for broadcasters, and especially those facing domestic competition, to feel that most news and public affairs programs must feature a large share of movement—and preferably colorful movement—in order to hold viewer attention.

Highly portable recording and transmission equipment has made it possible for journalists to obtain live or on-scene coverage of almost everything imaginable, and some things that are difficult to imagine: live ("real time") images of the allied bombardment of Baghdad during the Gulf War; on-scene footage of the police beating of Rodney King in Los Angeles and live coverage of the violent reactions to the first jury verdict in that case; Hindus destroying a Muslim temple in India in 1992. Once such coverage becomes technologically possible, broadcasters strive to use it. But it is expensive, so that it tends to feature amazing scenes of action, rather than images of reporters themselves attempting to describe it. If those reporters also bring some sense of perspective, especially in the form of qualification, to those scenes, they generally do so as disembodied voices accompanying the still-vivid visual depictions of scenes of action, which often are so powerful that they bury or negate any attempts at perspective. Furthermore, the instantaneous availability of action footage makes it quite tempting to let that footage "speak for itself," which it can only do in limited ways, and to let viewers "judge for themselves," which they can do only on the basis of limited evidence.

That is precisely why the reasoned judgment of experienced reporters and editors is so crucial to the responsible coverage of conflict: Compelling and amazing as it is, live action material badly needs the perspective and judgment that those individuals can provide, largely *because* the footage is so compelling and amazing. If viewers perceive it as the predominant element in the story, some may reject it because they regard it as nothing but vivid action without underlying significance, while others may accept it as an accurate and complete depiction of what is occurring, not just at that moment and in that location, but far more generally and significantly.

So much that comprises the overall phenomenon of conflict is not particularly visual, especially during its early stages. While there is some possibility that attempts made to cover it during those early stages may not attract much viewer attention, the effort is worthwhile. It will provide a base of understanding for some viewers, and it may educate others to the eventual point of realizing not only that they shouldn't expect visualization with every-thing, but also that there are circumstances where it may even obscure the most important elements of a story. In that respect, reporters and editors have an important educational role to play; in that and other respects, one can see why broadcast journalism is not a suitable profession for the faint-of-heart, indecisive, or irresponsible individual, and what tremendous responsibilities are borne by broad-cast journalists.

*Recognizing that stories attempting to explore the complexity of ethnic issues may not easily fit into the standard visual for-mat, the Commission on Radio and Televi-sion Policy recommended that stations "choose stories of the informative content rather than sensationalist pictures. If sta-tions choose to use highly dramatic and sensationalist pictures, as they often will, it is imperative that the television journalists provide suitable context and perspectives to accompany and explain such images."*

There is one circumstance involving conflict where very little of what is presented here has much prospect of being applied: open, declared war between two parties. The media generally become firm supporters of their respective governments, although they may take issue with specific decisions. Not only are they generally uncritical, but also they are sometimes willing to accept and even commit fabrication of "evidence" that supports the government's stance. Western reporters covering the long-running civil war in Burma have noted Burmese television's use of staged "atrocities" which were "committed" by Karin or other ethnic minorities opposing the government.

If reporters, editors, and broadcast administrators value their independence, as most do (or claim that they do), then clearly it is better for them to make every effort to cover events in ways that will head off conflict, or catch it in its early stages. If it erupts in open warfare, much if not all of that independence—the freedom to report fairly, openly, and evenhandedly—will vanish. Even Great Britain's BBC, with its strong tradition of fair and accurate reporting, quickly discovered in the Falklands War of 1982, that there were major costs in maintaining that tradition. A few BBC reports pointed out that grief over the loss of one's sons in battle was not limited to the British; a BBC reporter in Argentina even obtained interviews with weeping Argentinean parents whose sons had been killed. Those reports attracted heavy criticism from Prime Minister Margaret Thatcher, other Conservative Party members (and a few Labourites), and some British newspapers; the BBC was labeled as everything from "not a team player" to "disloyal" or even "treasonous." That relatively small burst of balance—most BBC reporting on the War was strongly pro-British—probably cost the BBC dearly in the long run, as the Conservative Party increased its efforts to place further restrictions on financial support and editorial freedom for the broadcaster.

# OBTAINING INFORMATION ABOUT ETHNIC GROUPS AND CONFLICT

As we noted in the discussion of conflict, having information ready at hand is crucial if coverage of it is to provide
balance, comprehensiveness, objectivity, and accuracy. A
detailed, up-to-date archive is very helpful, as is a comprehensive list of contacts: experts, spokespersons, etc. Staff
members with first-hand knowledge of specific groups,
sometimes on the basis of membership in them, also is
important. However, many groups are too small or obscure
to come to the attention of stations in that way. Still others,
especially the more militant organizations, are unlikely to
contain members who might be willing to, or would dare to,
leave the organization and work for a mainstream broadcast service. For example, it's doubtful that the Sri Lanka
Broadcasting Corporation would employ an ex-Tamil Ti-
ger, or that such an individual would feel safe from her or
his former colleagues after accepting such employment.

Those steps tell us little about the process of obtaining
information about groups, aside from working with staff
who may be familiar with them. And even there, many
groups will go "unrepresented," often because they don't
wish to make themselves known, at least until they choose
to do so. Strategies for obtaining information cannot be
developed or applied formulaically, but the following observations may help to suggest possible lines of approach.

*Governments,* whether local, regional, or national, are major sources of information on conflict and ethnic minorities in most countries. (The military and law enforcement agencies also are major sources of information on conflict, and the latter often is an important source on ethnic minorities. However, neither one is elected to office, and may find it easier to refuse to divulge information than do elected government officials.) Sometimes their output exists in undigested form, requiring the user to go through hundreds of pages to find useful data, if it is not already indexed. Sometimes it is carefully packaged, so that it will be ready for media use—written in appropriate language, timed or measured so that it can be inserted as part or all of a newscast item or newspaper article. And if it is skillfully prepared (governments frequently employ experienced journalists), it can lead reporters and editors to feel that it is ready for use without further alteration, which is convenient for the media (time is always in short supply) and for the government (it may be able to avoid facing embarrassing questions).

Where conflict and ethnic minority relations are concerned, however, government units often have reasons for disclosing less than they know. They might justify less than full disclosure in the name of order, efficiency, safety, security, and any of a host of other reasons. They might also wish to keep the media more dependent upon them by doling out information in piecemeal fashion, so as to remind media staff of who is in control. Also, they may be selective in handing out information, providing more of it to specific media operations that they can "trust." That sort of selectivity also can be used to play media organizations off against one another. And they may attempt to protect their top administrators by adopting a confrontational attitude: "That's all you're going to get for now. No further questions."

There are ways of getting around some of the barriers, ranging from cultivation of personal acquaintances within the units to seeking release of classified information through "freedom of information" acts, if they exist. However, very few countries have them, whereas acts sanctioning government *protection* of information are quite common. Furthermore, obtaining results through freedom of information acts can be highly time-consuming and expensive, since gaining access usually involves searching through a large body of material, often not indexed, to see whether it contains useful elements. Sometimes it is even necessary to pay for the copying of the entire file before combing through it.

The main point to bear in mind when working with government units on issues involving conflict and ethnic minorities is to remember that, complete as the information they furnish may seem to be, it is almost inevitable that one will have to go beyond it if one is to have any hope of preparing a balanced and comprehensive, or even accurate, account. Once in possession of such information, a reporter is in a good position to turn to former government officials (and military or law enforcement personnel) who were connected with a given event at an earlier time. Many such individuals, once they are aware that a reporter is well-informed on the subject, will be more than ready to provide their insider's views on the event.

*Spokespersons for groups* are essential in this media age, and even small ethnic groups may have them. Sometimes they are the sole channel through which a group will communicate with the media; other group members may be under strict orders not to communicate anything to "outsiders," including (and perhaps especially) the media. Even when that is not the case, it usually is much simpler for media personnel to work with spokespersons, who are accessible, at ease working with the media, able to prepare information in a form that is readily usable, and often speak

65

with authority—particularly when, as often is the case, they also happen to be leaders of their groups.

Again, as with government officials, it seems wise to develop other sources of information from within the groups, although doing so can be difficult or even dangerous. Contact with former group members can be helpful, provided that the reporter can distinguish information that is related to personal grudges against one or a few group members, but may not characterize the group as a whole. It also is important for reporters to beware of becoming unwitting pawns in internal power struggles. Information gathered as a result of such internal conflict may be useful, but it also can provide a misleading picture of group cohesiveness, goals, and methods.

*Scholars in universities and research institutes* who study conflict and ethnic groups are fairly obvious choices when looking for information. Here, it is essential to determine the sources used most prominently in their research. If much of their material is old, if only a few sources are used, or if the scholar has very strong personal feelings about the subject, caution is necessary. And, while most of their research is physically accessible, it may not always be readily understandable to the general public.

*Religious authorities,* such as rabbis, priests, imams, and monks, frequently are very well qualified to offer useful viewpoints, and perhaps factual information, on conflict and on ethnic minorities. In cases where religion is a major element in the conflict, as in Lebanon, Bosnia, Sudan, Armenia, Azerbaijan, and many other places, it is essential to obtain such viewpoints, but rarely will they be disinterested views. Religious authorities are more likely than many other sources to have a real sense of history, and can provide reams of it, but again, it is apt to be quite selective.

***Business personnel*** are good sources on the economic dimensions of conflict and of ethnic minority affairs. They often are better (for the purposes of broadcasters and their audiences) than economists, because they can explain in clear, simple, and human terms such things as the difficulties faced by ethnic minorities when attempting to reestablish businesses following a major disorder, or situations faced by businesses in terms of complying with statutes on hiring practices, subcontracting, etc., where ethnic minorities are concerned.

***Doctors and other health professionals*** often are well-suited to conveying the human dimensions of conflict and ethnic minority experiences. Their descriptions may be, if anything, too graphic in depicting the truly miserable situations faced by individuals, families, and larger groups caught up in conflict or deprived of access to needed help because of their ethnicity. But at least they are unlikely to withhold information.

***Other sources,*** some of them quite unconventional, may be worth considering. For example, artists can bring interesting perspectives to bear on conflict and on the lives led by ethnic minorities. As their forms of expression almost always are aural and/or visual, they are "naturals" for broadcasting. One might not turn to them for basic information, but they can bring dimensions to stories that may help audiences, minority and majority alike, to empathize more readily.

There also are the less obvious, but directly observable, signs of growing discontent or even emerging conflict. Graffiti, wall posters, popular songs, rallies, and leaflets were noted earlier. There are still others, such as religious addresses (the Ayatollah Khomeini and his followers made effective use of his recorded anti-Shah sermons, which were dupli-

67

cated and distributed throughout Iran in the late 1970s), counter-culture comic books, stand-up comedy and satire, and plays (Beaumarchais' *Figaro* trilogy often is regarded as one of the more important harbingers of the French revolution). There also are mass media sources, such as ethnic minority newspapers, magazines, and broadcast stations. U.S. radio stations in particular have become prominent as sources of "community feelings" expressed through talk shows. Such shows may have played a positive role in Los Angeles immediately following the initial "not guilty" verdict in the Rodney King case, in that they appeared to serve as a "safety valve" through which callers could vent their anger.

All of those sources, and more, are of potential value, but the electronic media tend to turn to them only after situations have reached the crisis point or conflict has broken out openly. Reporters should turn to them for information and opinion at other times, if only so that their appearance on air isn't always associated with open crisis or overt conflict. However, staff members may need occasional reminders to do so.

*One excellent way of providing such reminders is the creation of advisory boards made up of a cross-section of the citizenry. The Commission, noting that the autonomy and independence of the journalistic enterprise was paramount, expressed concern that television stations be enabled to assess their policies and gain information from audiences. The Commission recommended the establishment of "advisory boards of ethnic and community leaders who are not representatives of the government, to meet at least quarterly with management of the television station to address and evaluate issues of coverage."*

Many national broadcasting services, particularly the public service organizations in Europe, as well as a number of regional and local broadcasters, have created such boards. Great Britain has had long experience with them, and frequently established them in its colonies, which in some cases, e.g., India, have continued them. Most of the northern European countries have them. A typical board has from 15 to 50 members, who usually are chosen by the broadcasters themselves; that may not be the best guarantee of independence of judgment, and the German system requires societal groups themselves—unions, religious organizations, teachers, etc.—to select members. (However, the German boards make no provision for representation of ethnic minorities—mainly "guest workers" and immigrants.)

Such boards usually meet three or four times a year, ordinarily for no more than a full working day, although members and broadcasters can petition for additional meetings, if they feel the need. They review the overall record of the previous three months, discuss what is proposed for the next three months, raise questions on anything they wish, request special reports on certain subjects (broadcast policy on violence, depiction of ethnic minorities in prime-time drama, etc.), and question broadcaster decisions, at liberty. They have no veto power over decisions, but they often can and do publicize their deliberations through the mass media. Oddly enough, the broadcasters they advise are not required to carry reports of those deliberations, and many do not. Broadcasters explain this seeming omission by claiming that, if the deliberations are positive where broadcasting is concerned—and often they are—audiences might come to feel that the boards are mere rubber stamps or lap dogs. Broadcasters also claim that such nonpublicity helps to keep board members from being "pestered" by the public to support one or another position.

Therefore, the boards really do not directly represent the public, except insofar as their individual members might have a reasonably good sense of public moods and tastes. Their ultimate value to the broadcaster and to society lies in the quality of independence of those members, and the extent to which the broadcaster will seriously consider what they recommend. There is no way to ensure absolutely any of that by law, although the broadcast laws of some of the German states do give such boards the power to hire and fire the station manager and to accept or reject certain parts of station budgets. The German practice of requiring societal groups to appoint members probably helps to ensure greater independence of judgment, as well. And it would seem wise to place term limits on board member appointments, as most boards do: three years, in most cases, and renewable.

Requiring broadcasters to carry board reports of deliberations and recommendations probably would help to ensure even greater independence of judgment, especially if it encouraged audience members who are disturbed by broadcaster coverage of conflict and of ethnic minority affairs to urge board members to raise questions and call for investigation of such subjects. The board reports themselves need not be dry, "talking heads" summaries; they can be illustrated by video clips of elements that certain audience and board members may have found offensive, distasteful, but also provocative, or inspirational.

If broadcast staff are to make maximum use of board recommendations, it is essential that management share those deliberations with the production staff who might logically be expected to act upon them. But that will not be sufficient; management also must indicate that it takes the recommendations seriously, and will be looking to see what the production staff have done with them. It is quite easy for staff to take the attitude, "That's just public relations. We're professionals, we know what we're doing, and we don't need another set of opinions, especially when we're attempting to cover fast-moving conflict or complex ethnic minority issues." There is some truth to that claim, and certainly management would not be wise to press every single board recommendation on the staff. Still, boards can serve as a *vox populi* of sorts, and can bring an audience perspective to the attention of producers and others who may have become so caught up in the process of production that they may forget or minimize the audience impact of what they produce. If board members are realistic, they will be aware that financial, technical, and other considerations may rule out implementation of some of their recommendations.

In the final analysis, most members serve because they truly want to help broadcasters in the latter's desire (ideally, at any rate) to build healthy societies. If broadcasters will take the advice offered by boards in that spirit, then a genuine and fruitful collaboration will be the result—to everyone's benefit.

Because board members often are prominent members of society (labor union leaders, noted religious figures, etc.), they also can serve as useful sources of information, both about their own occupations and about the circles in which they move. Some countries have general advisory boards and a number of specialized boards, e.g., for children's programming, for religious programming. If there are boards for ethnic minority issues in broadcasting—they are rare, although the BBC has one for Asian programming—such board members can be even more useful, which may be a good argument for creating more of them. However, care should be taken to see to it that boards dealing with ethnic minority affairs not become isolated from the overall context of broadcast programming, management, and employment. A major goal, and possibly *the* major goal, of broadcasters and of those who advise them should be to ensure that coverage of ethnic minority affairs and conflict be furnished in ways that will enlighten all of society.

There is one further form of information-gathering that demands attention: *research conducted by broadcasters themselves.* One form of research—gathering information about potential conflicts and ethnic minorities—has been covered already. In fact, some would argue that it should not be called research because it is not truly scientific or methodical. A second form of research—gathering information about audience size, composition, and reactions to programming—certainly can be scientific and methodical, although that is not always the case.

Most large electronic media operations have research departments. Some of them conduct a wide range of research, while others confine themselves to "counting noses" in order to learn how many of what sorts of people watched or listened to what kinds of programming. The latter can be valuable, but is particularly lacking where operations need data on such highly subjective matters as reactions to programming about conflicts and ethnic minorities.

Such programming, as noted in the preface, is by definition a complex issue. Quantitative data on audience size and composition will aid broadcasters in determining whether particular subgroups within the overall audience—older men, viewers with no more than six years of formal education, specific ethnic minorities—have been reached in significant numbers. In addition, many European broadcasters use numerically based audience appreciation indexes, which reveal on scales of 1–10 or A–F how highly audiences regarded specific programs. But audience comprehension, interpretation, and sense of impact are at least as important as popularity. And *why* viewers or listeners understand or don't understand what producers hoped they would understand, or why audience members feel some real impact or do not, all must be considered by broadcasters if such programming is to be effective.

Qualitative research, whether conducted in laboratory studies, with focus groups, or through individual interviews, is costly. It also can be slow to collect and to process, which makes it difficult for broadcasters to use in times of crisis, when they want answers quickly. Still, if electronic media managers place a high enough budgetary priority on audience research, and insist that program producers are to take it seriously, researchers often can produce preliminary results within a matter of days, provided that they have worked closely enough with producers over time to be able to anticipate some of their needs.

There is one important issue where research on ethnic minority viewing and listening is concerned. Ethnic minority audience members often are underrepresented in qualitative (as well as quantitative) studies: They often are more difficult to contact than are members of the majority culture; they may prove less cooperative, due to suspicions about the uses to which the research will be put, but also due to cynicism as to the value to them of participating in such studies. Quantitative and qualitative research organizations in the United States, Nielsen and The Arbitron Company in particular, have gone to considerable lengths (greater financial inducements to participate, use of more ethnic minority staff to contact ethnic minority households) to increase levels of ethnic minority representation in their overall samples of U.S. households, but such representation continues to be a problem.

Audience research can be carried out within the broadcast organization, but increasing numbers of broadcasters—Germany and Great Britain are major examples—work through independent research bodies much of the time. That helps to reassure the public that the broadcasters themselves are not designing, executing, or interpreting the research in ways that will make them look good, or will avoid the difficult issues. However, carefully executed research is its own best guarantee of quality. Media managers acting on the basis of its findings and sharing those findings with the public will be the best possible guarantee of its importance.

In that process, it is crucial for managers to ask themselves the truly difficult questions. It is equally crucial for them to work with researchers to ensure that the public can respond frankly to such questions—no small feat in countries where frank answers to questions on sensitive issues once were an almost certain way to invite the unwelcome attention of the authorities. Media autonomy from those authorities should reassure the public that its trust in the media is not misplaced.

# RECRUITMENT AND TRAINING

*The Commission on Radio and Television Policy recommended that stations have "training opportunities for minority employees and actively attract participants." In order to ensure a vigorous program of minority recruitment, the Commission recommended that "a high-ranking member of station management should have the responsibility for identifying and hiring minority group members at all levels of employment for both sides of the camera—editorial as well as managerial positions."*

The electronic media seldom have problems in attracting staff members who have a strong interest in the coverage of conflict. Major conflicts such as Watergate, or the civil war in Bosnia, often are followed by increased interest on the part of students and others to become journalists. They may be attracted by the prospect of becoming famous, they may feel that investigative reporting is an important cure for the ills of society, or they may think the media needs better balance in their portrayal of society. However, those who are attracted usually turn out to be members of the majority culture.

Several studies in North America, Europe, and Australia have shown that ethnic minorities are not particularly visible in the mainstream electronic media, and certainly not as staff members. As noted in Chapter One, very few media organizations paid any serious attention to ethnic minority situations, languages, or employment until the 1970s or 1980s. Memories are long, and ethnic minorities still may wonder how much difference they could make if they were to secure positions in mainstream media. Also, there are increasing numbers of ethnic minority radio stations, which may serve as more congenial outlets for their talents, far from the mainstream though they may be. There may be more lucrative employment available through law, medicine, government service, business, the military, or law enforcement, and many of those occupations offer more rapid advancement than does broadcasting. Finally, ethnic minority individuals who are among the few, or even sole, representatives of their particular minority groups on mainstream channels run the risk of attracting criticism from their peers for having been "co-opted" by the majority culture, particularly if they appear to function as nothing more than darker- or lighter-skinned, differently accented versions of mainstream newscasters, actors, program hosts, or announcers.

*Recruitment:* Any sincere effort at recruitment of ethnic minority staff by mainstream broadcasters must recognize that there may be a fair amount of skepticism to be overcome. Probably the best place to begin to dispel that skepticism is with visible indications in the programming—news, entertainment, advertising—that mainstream television and radio are becoming more sensitive to ethnic minority experiences. Results will not be immediately apparent. Decades of neglect, earlier false hopes, are not quickly forgotten. Broadcasting in many countries has undergone brief periods of increased sensitivity (often called "relevance"), only to slip back into its former ways when the

76

popularity of "relevant" programs declined. Majority society also sometimes has become more openly hostile toward such increases. That may be because it regards the new programming as overly gentle in its treatment of minorities—overly ready to seem to excuse or even ignore what many in majority society regard as offensive or even criminal. Thus, ethnic minorities are likely to reserve judgment until the changes do seem more or less permanent this time, and the opportunities presented appear both meaningful and rewarding.

Recruiting of ethnic minority broadcast staff ideally should begin with school systems. The final section of this monograph will advocate greater media involvement with schools where critical appreciation of programs is concerned. But increased contact with schools also can provide increased contact with ethnic minorities, and broadcasters can attempt to instill in young students a vision of their futures as reporters, producers, managers, writers, and performers. While children appear to be showing signs of cynicism at earlier and earlier ages, they still seem to harbor a reservoir of trust, compassion, and desire to make the world a better place, for their own ethnic groups and for humankind in general.

However, recruitment at that level should not unduly emphasize minorities. Majority cultures usually retain their primacy over time, at least on a national level. Therefore, much good can come of bringing *all* children to understand that the electronic media can serve as powerful agents for social change, and that all of them can play important roles in seeing to it that it be change for the better for *all* societal groups. Furthermore, there are ways to ensure such an outcome whether one is employed by a media organization or not. The larger public can help to shape media output in various positive ways: writing letters of praise or criticism of media output; cooperating in surveys; educating their own children to be more perceptive and demanding media consumers; helping with fund-raising drives for community radio and TV stations; contributing time as volunteers for such stations; and making programs for access TV.

Most primary schools in the United States, and some in Europe (especially in northern Europe) have "career days" in which students meet with representatives of various occupations. The electronic media should become actively involved in those events, but should be careful to represent themselves through more than just ethnic minority staff, if there are any, so as to avoid charges of displaying "token" minorities. Many secondary schools have classes dealing with preparation for possible careers, and some have their own media facilities, including wired (for in-school distribution) radio stations; TV production gear; and modest studios, which may be linked with a local cable TV system. Active participation by mainstream broadcast personnel in such efforts—as guest critics, as auxiliary instructors, as donors of used equipment, as technical advisors—will help to develop a greater atmosphere of trust and interest on the part of all students, and may lead some of them to feel that broadcasting really might be an attractive career.

Much the same holds true for contact with trade schools, colleges, and universities, with one major difference: While it is rare for a broadcaster to provide internships or apprenticeships for primary or secondary school students, it is quite common where tertiary students are concerned. They usually have the physical appearance and vocal maturity to serve as on-air talent, and possibly even the career motivation to take an internship or apprenticeship seriously—and, therefore, the willingness to commit the time to the experience week after week, month after month. That commitment will seem even more worthwhile if interns are paid, as some media organizations do. Some governments, too, make money available for broadcasters to pay interns; New Zealand, for one, has financed internships of various sorts, including broadcasting, for Maori youth. Some commercial radio stations in Great Britain have financed summer internships, as well; there, interns usually are assigned to a particular staff member, who becomes their mentor for the summer, and helps them to develop broadcast-worthy productions.

College and university radio stations (rare outside industrially developed nations) also can be good recruiting grounds for ethnic minority talent, especially when the institutions themselves feature a particular minority population. However, that may be a sensitive issue: If ethnic minority stations already exist, or if there are plans for them, their managers may resent mainstream "raiding" of what they see as an important talent pool for themselves.

One of the more abundant sources of potential ethnic minority recruits, and experienced recruits, at that, is in the staff of already-existing stations and networks. Such staff are quite likely to find a new position attractive so long as it really represents increased opportunity, and not just a token hire of a "visible" minority. Print media also can be excellent sources of talent, and not only for journalists: managers, sales personnel, and others often will have highly transferable experience. Again, broadcasters should observe the caveat regarding any perception of "raiding," which is an especially sensitive point here: Most mainstream broadcast operations can outspend minority media operations by a wide margin and can offer salaries that are hard to decline.

Finally, there have been a few attempts at combining minority recruitment and formal training in a way that might attract ethnic minority individuals with a diverse set of educational and life-experience backgrounds. The U.S. National Association for the Advancement of Colored People

(NAACP) made a major effort in the course of its 1963 annual convention to pressure broadcasters and the movie industry to open their doors to African-American staff, both on-air and behind the scenes. In 1964, the National Urban League, working with the three U.S. commercial television networks, set up a training program called the Broadcast Skills Bank. It included a prescreening of African-Americans (it began to include other minorities later on) to determine their apparent aptitude for some form of broadcast work, as well as their commitment to it. Those accepted were assured that, if they passed a several-month-long training course, they would be guaranteed a job by the network with which they had trained. (Training usually took place at network facilities, and the networks covered the costs of the program itself.) Many did pass, and moved into network positions. There was occasional resentment over the fact that some individuals had to move to another city if they wanted jobs, but on the whole the Skills Bank experience led to favorable outcomes. After several years, the networks began to operate the program through colleges and universities, and guarantees of positions became less certain, although many still materialized. By the early 1970s, the Bank was largely a thing of the past, although some colleges and universities carry out media workshops for prospective ethnic minority media staff to this day.

During the mid-1980s, an ILR station in Great Britain, Cardiff Broadcasting Company, operated a training program which was intended to interest members of various ethnic minority groups in pursuing careers in radio. From the time of its founding in 1983, the Cardiff station had been far more interested in encouraging a real sense of community involvement than were most ILR stations. A combination of private foundation (Gulbenkian) grants and some assistance from ILR headquarters in London made it possible for the station to hire a Black trainer, Junior Stephens, and to pay trainees a modest stipend for the time they spent in the project. Initial reaction by the trainees was enthusiastic, largely because the training was very practical and thorough; a few subsequently found positions in stations around the country. However, funding ran out after two years, and the program was discontinued. The Afro-Caribbean Radio Project in Brixton, a largely Black district in south London, was established in 1987 and supported by members of the Afro-Caribbean community themselves to provide practical training for prospective Black broadcasters. However, as the organization had no radio station, trainees produced tapes in a studio in order to simulate on-air broadcasting.

The Broadcast Skills Bank, the Cardiff program, and the Afro-Caribbean Radio Project concentrated largely on the training of production personnel and certain categories of on-air talent: sports, weather, news presentation, but not dramatic acting. Directing and producing programs received less attention, and management virtually none. The lack of management training has been noted by a number of groups and individuals who have tried to get the U.S. broadcast media to improve their portrayal of ethnic minorities. The chief criticism was summed up quite well in the 1977 and 1979 reports ("Window Dressing on the Set") of the U.S. Commission on Civil Rights. The Commission pointed out the heavily stereotyped nature of ethnic minority roles in many entertainment shows (where certain minorities, such as Native Americans, were virtually invisible), but also the low numbers of ethnic minority broadcast journalists, the scant coverage of ethnic minority-related news items, and the almost total absence of ethnic minority individuals as "expert" (or even "lay") interviewees on newscasts, interview, or panel shows. They attributed this neglect in part to the lack of ethnic minority decision-makers in broadcasting. Without such decision-makers, especially in the networks, ethnic minority viewpoints and even presence were bound to suffer neglect, benign or otherwise. While there were no guarantees that ethnic minority decision-makers would correct that imbalance, the assumption was that they could have some effect on it, sooner or later.

*Training:* With the exception of the already-well-experienced recruit, stations and networks will have to spend some time, effort, and money in the training of staff. (Even in smaller stations, where new personnel are infrequent enough that they can learn on the job, there will be some investment of time and effort.) Any training program should include attention to human (social) as well as professional integration in the media operation. That is no simple task: some majority culture staff will resent what they see as preferential treatment of ethnic minorities, and some ethnic minorities will mistake the sometimes brusque and even harsh criticism of their performance by majority culture staff as ethnic discrimination. It may be, but it also may be due to the often hectic pace of broadcasting. That hectic pace itself sometimes leads to another problem: Majority culture staff may continue to do certain jobs themselves, rather than show new recruits how to do them, just because it saves time. That usually produces an inadequately trained staff member, which can perpetuate stereotypes like, "This is just one more sign that minorities can't do the job as well as we can." Problems of that sort can be avoided, or more readily rectified, if station management meets regularly with staff and trainees to assess progress within the program.

It also would help if, during the training process itself, ethnic minority trainees could serve as resources on ethnic minority situations. As resource persons, minorities are more likely to feel that they are contributing, as well as receiving. They also can gain some measure of status in the process, provided that they are truly well-informed. However, stations must not regard trainees as informers, which could discredit them as well as the station, and could even be dangerous for them.

Mainstream staff members also could profit from training as a part of the process of speeding up integration. They will learn something from working with ethnic minority recruits, but they also should be urged to attend relevant courses, if any are available, at local schools; there they could learn more about sources of discrimination, different lifestyles, and even possibly minority languages. The New Zealand Broadcasting Corporation has had a Maori language program in place for several years. It is free of charge to all NZBC staff wishing to take it. While virtually all Maori, and especially those in broadcasting, are bilingual, the Corporation hopes that learning the language will give majority culture staff a greater understanding of, and respect for, Maori culture.

# 7

# ENFORCEMENT MECHANISMS

It is always best if an electronic media operation can create its own means of ensuring the standard of performance that it has set for itself, so that the impulse to succeed comes from within. Unfortunately, that does not always happen. Financial pressures, shortages of properly trained personnel, "blind spots" (failure to perceive one's own shortcomings), and even tolerance for, or deliberate attempts at, the use of the media to increase ethnic tension and promote conflict all can lead to broadcasts which are not in the best interests of a healthy society. That also leads to a need for regulation—a need which is met in various ways.

*Self-regulation* often is cited as the ideal way to bring broadcasters to carry out their responsibilities to society. Doctors, lawyers, and others regulate themselves to a considerable degree, sometimes taking such drastic actions as limiting what their errant peers will be allowed to do, or even removing entirely their privileges of practicing medicine or the law. In theory, those most directly connected with a profession will have the greatest knowledge of it, are in the best position to determine when its standards have not been upheld, and have the most to gain from maintaining them.

Electronic media in many countries have tried their hands at self-regulation through professional associations.

Commercial broadcasters in Japan, Australia, New Zealand, Canada, the United States, and elsewhere have organized themselves through national associations. That simplifies the exchange of information among them, but it also gives them a forum for the discussion of mutual problems. Some of them develop "codes of good practice" for their mutual guidance, and certain of those codes contain provisions regarding ethnic minorities. For example, the U.S. National Association of Broadcasters (NAB) Television Code, while it was still in force (it was suspended in 1983), stated, "Special sensitivity is necessary in the use of material relating to sex, race, color, age, creed, religious functionaries or rites, or national or ethnic derivation." Such a generalized statement is not likely to be of much help to a station manager. Nor does it give the association itself very specific grounds for disciplining a member, presuming the association had any disciplinary powers, as many do not.

A few of the associations have addressed the under-representation of ethnic minorities; the NAB's Office of Minority Affairs prods stations to offer internships, increase hiring, and help new stations run by ethnic minorities. However, most associations spend most of their time on other matters—chiefly, how to keep the governments of their respective countries from increasing the level of governmental regulation. Minority broadcasting is a minor, or even nonexistent, issue, for many of them. Japanese broadcasters, for example, almost totally ignore the nation's several hundred thousand Korean residents. Broadcasting's coverage of conflict in society, whether or not it relates to ethnic minorities, receives little or no discussion in the conventions, newsletters, or other outlets of such broadcaster associations.

Reporters, editors, and news and public affairs administrators sometimes have their own professional associations, such as the British National Union of Journalists or the U.S. Radio-Television News Directors Association (RTNDA). As groups of broadcasters on the front line of the coverage of conflict, those associations can take some helpful steps in exchanging information and even setting general guidelines or standards of performance for such coverage. For example, the Philippine Press Institute's Journalist's Code of Ethics (1991) states, "I shall not in any manner ridicule, cast aspersions on, or degrade any person by reason of sex, creed, religious belief, political conviction, cultural or ethnic origin."

Like many of the national associations just mentioned, these associations usually are voluntary. There usually are no enforcement mechanisms to ensure compliance with agreed-upon standards of conduct, aside from the moral influence that professionals can have on one another, which sometimes is quite effective. A few associations, such as the Philippine Broadcasters' Association, have a schedule of fines and of periods of suspension from PBA membership. The NUJ and the RTNDA both have made pronouncements about the need for better understanding and presentation of ethnic minority perspectives, and the RTNDA has made scholarships available to ethnic minority students considering careers in broadcast journalism.

Many of the public service broadcast operations, and some commercial stations and networks, practice self-regulation through internally developed codes of conduct and guidelines for staff. Such codes and guidelines are especially common in news and public affairs divisions; the BBC and Independent Television News in Great Britain, the Canadian Broadcasting Corporation, ARD and ZDF in Germany, and many others have specific codes and guidelines on permissible, questionable, and even impermissible terminology, especially as it applies to ethnic minorities, but also in connection with the coverage of conflict. Because these codes and guidelines are developed by the very broadcasters who use them, they are usually observed. There is the possibility that broadcasters may miss certain subtleties or nuances in terminology, but such codes and guidelines usually receive the inspection of members of ethnic minority and other relevant communities, and their suggestions may be incorporated with the final version of the document.

*Governmental regulation,* especially through an agency established for that purpose (France's Conseil Superieure de l'Audiovisuel; the Canadian Radio-Television and Telecommunications Commission), or through a designated ministry (Malaysia's Ministry of Information; Sudan's Ministry of Information and Culture), may be quite effective in holding the electronic media to specific standards of performance. Under some circumstances, they may be absolutely repressive, as is the case with Sudan. Such agencies and ministries usually have the power to grant and rescind broadcast licenses, the latter on the basis of serious violation of regulations. Regulations may or may not be detailed, but ordinarily they contain little that is specific about coverage of conflict and ethnic minorities. Instead, agencies and ministries work through existing criminal law, for example on penalties for incitement to riot, or equal (nondiscriminatory) employment legislation. For example, Singapore's Consultative Committee on Censorship in the Ministry of Information and the Arts sees to it that the electronic media follow the country's censorship laws, especially regarding violence and pornography. The Consultative Committee appears to be having some success in bringing the government—long known for following a policy of very strict censorship—to relax those restrictions a bit.

A few regulatory agencies have attempted to increase the sheer number of stations operated by ethnic minorities through some sort of preferential licensing policy. The U.S. FCC initiated such a policy in 1973, and has enlarged it since then. One provision allows the Commission to give preference to ethnic minority applicants in cases where there is competition for a given license and the competitors are roughly equal in terms of meeting basic FCC criteria, such as local ownership. Another allows ethnic minority applicants two drawings instead of one in the lottery system used to issue licenses for low-power television stations. Numbers of African-American-owned stations have increased to the point where a national organization (the National Association of Black-Owned Broadcasters) now helps to represent their interests.

Regulatory agencies in other countries have developed different approaches to the licensing of minority-owned, or at least -oriented, services. Great Britain's newly created (1990) Radio Authority licensed several West Indian, South Asian, and other ethnic minority stations between 1991 and 1993, but without any overt preference policy. Its counterpart for television, satellite, and cable, the Television Authority, licensed in 1992 a satellite-to-cable TV service headquartered in London. The Middle East Broadcasting Centre transmits news and entertainment in Arabic to the Middle East, but it also is receivable in Great Britain. The Netherlands Media Authority has approved the retransmission from satellite to cable of television programs from Turkey's TRT, which has been welcomed by the many Turks living in the Netherlands.

Those and other developments have increased the amount of ethnic minority (especially linguistic minority) programming. But not everyone—and particularly not the less well-off guest workers and migrants, as well as long-resident ethnic minorities—can afford to subscribe to cable or satellite services. Furthermore, if the services are in languages other than those spoken by the majority culture, mainstream society will derive little benefit from whatever diversity those services provide. Also, to repeat a point raised earlier, mainstream services may claim that they no longer need to cover ethnic minority affairs, since these new services do the job. Again, mainstream audiences will miss out on potentially useful information.

Regulatory agencies also may undertake studies of broadcast practices, or of public reactions to programming, and then issue the findings publicly. The hope is that, if study results reflect poorly on broadcasters, the latter will respond by correcting their behaviors. In 1992, the Australian Broadcasting Authority surveyed public attitudes toward television's portrayal of ethnic minorities. Majority culture viewers were not terribly disturbed about what they acknowledged as underrepresentation of ethnic minorities; minorities themselves were quite unhappy about it. It will be the difficult task of the ABA to translate this into a policy which would help to rectify the imbalance.

During the 1980s, several European nations, as well as New Zealand, followed the North American lead and "deregulated" broadcasting and cable so as to promote the growth of each. However, such diversity of ownership as has developed has been of only limited assistance to ethnic minorities, either as owners or as faces and voices on the air. Certainly there has been growth in the number of stations and, in some countries, cable operations, but almost all of it has been in the form of commercially supported activity targeted to majority culture audiences. Few of the new stations are run by unpaid volunteers on a nonprofit basis, although nonprofit radio stations in France—a number of which offer programming especially for linguistic (Basque, Provençal, Breton) or ethnic (Arab in particular) minorities—receive a subvention from the government. Instead, most of the newer stations operate on a highly competitive commercial basis, for the most part:

Many of them offer little or no news coverage, while popular music, much of it delivered nationally, by satellite, dominates the schedule.

The regulatory agencies could have established licensing conditions for the newer stations that would have required transmission of specified amounts of news, ethnic minority programming, etc. However, that would have run counter to the impulses that had led to the deregulation of broadcasting in the first place. Much of that movement was driven by economic philosophies held by government leaders: U.S. President Ronald Reagan, German Chancellor Helmut Kohl, British Prime Minister Margaret Thatcher, and many others. They, and their economic advisers, felt strongly that an "opening up" of the competitive market would be good for many types of business enterprises, and would stimulate their respective economies. The result was that the regulatory agencies were discouraged from setting standards for performance that would have mandated or at least encouraged better or more coverage of conflict and ethnic minorities, because that would discourage new applicants and hold down economic growth. Instead, new license holders often sought to compete largely on the basis of reducing programming costs, and not on the alternative forms of programming that they might provide. News and public affairs programming is particularly expensive, and many of the new stations never have provided it, although there are several news and public affairs services (CNN, C-SPAN, Sky News, n-TV) available through cable or direct from satellite in North America and Europe. Nor are ethnic minority-oriented programs particularly attractive to advertisers, aside from occasional "hits" such as the U.S. *The Cosby Show*. They may appear on cable access programs in the largest European cities, such as Berlin, but they are quite scarce elsewhere.

91

Some of the regulatory agencies have withdrawn regulations that had been of some assistance to ethnic minorities wishing to improve their portrayal by the electronic media, but also to bring about more balanced coverage of conflict. As noted earlier, the FCC had a Fairness Doctrine since 1949; it had allowed individuals and groups to seek reply time to respond to what they regarded as one-sided, unfair, or distorted broadcasts. The Commission dropped the Doctrine in 1987, partly as a response to broad-casters who claimed that it inhibited them from dealing with controversial issues where they might be faced with many demands for reply time. But the Commission also reasoned that there were plenty of broadcast outlets available, and thus, ample means for replying to such messages, even if the "offending" broadcaster itself would not agree to broadcast the reply. That is of little help to anyone living in an area served by one or two stations, of course, especially if the stations are owned and operated by individuals with strongly held viewpoints which they promote over the air, sometimes through a barrage of advertising, and which they are unwilling to "weaken" by giving or selling opponents any airtime.

*Legislatures* also become directly involved in broadcast regulation. Most of them appropriate the annual budgets for the regulatory agencies, and establish the legislation under which the agencies function. Many have standing legislative committees on broadcasting. In the past, regulation of the mass media was not often a major concern of legislators. However, crises in society, seemingly more numerous in recent years, and often involving conflict and ethnic minorities, have led to an increase in legislator interest. Charges that the mass media have played negative roles covering crises have stimulated legislators to hold special hearings, issue reports, and threaten the media with increased regulation. That rarely materializes, in part because legislators lack persistence, in part because many of them believe in self-regulation and in open competition. Also, the electronic media can be important "friends" for politicians, who welcome as much favorable media attention as they can get. Politicians are not apt to be overcritical of such friends. However, the U.S. inner-city disturbances (Watts, Detroit, Newark) of the mid-1960s brought strong legislator reactions; so did the commission of exceptionally brutal crimes by juveniles in Great Britain, some against ethnic minorities, in the early 1990s.

Still, most legislators would rather develop close working relationships with the media than penalize them for their errors of omission and commission (although legislators are happy enough to criticize their practices, since that is a virtual guarantee of publicity). Parliamentary deliberation in India eventually led to the passage of a new broadcasting act in the early 1990s, but there is little confidence that Congress Party political influence on broadcasting will abate, or that All India Radio or Doordarshan (TV) will improve their records of covering conflict within Indian society fairly and completely. The British Parliament, or rather, its Conservative majority, had somewhat greater success in getting the BBC and Independent (commercial) Broadcasting to limit their coverage of conflict in Northern Ireland and activities of the IRA, but the Conservatives had the advantage of a high degree of party unity on the issue, considerable popular support, and control of the size of the annual license fee which provides most of the BBC's financial support.

Legislatures in the eastern European nations and the new states that have emerged from the former Soviet Union have had the opportunity to prepare brand-new media laws. However, few of them have managed to do so thus far. In Poland, the legislators split over the issue of whether all broadcasters should be required to feature a "Roman Catholic point of view" through their programming. Advocates of birth control, as well as religious minorities—Jewish and Russian Orthodox—in Poland, would find such a provision most unsettling. Legislatures in Bulgaria, Hungary, and elsewhere in the region seem ready enough to authorize the licensing of private broadcast stations (there are many unlicensed stations on the air already, and they exhibit little fear that the authorities will remove them anytime soon). However, there is a large roadblock to the passage of laws that would make formal authorization possible: How can laws be written so as to exclude certain parties from eligibility? Legislators express fears over massive investment by outsiders (already the French, Italians, Germans, Turks, British, Americans, Canadians, and others are involved), ownership by ethnic minorities (Hungarians in Rumania, Turks in Bulgaria, etc.), and especially involvement on the part of former Communists (many of whom still hold high positions in the state-run broadcast services). Freedom of speech receives much praise when legislators and other political leaders discuss it in the abstract, but that praise often is qualified when new broadcast laws are up for consideration.

Where the legislative branch is at odds with the executive, the state is set for a political duel, in which the prize is often control of television and radio. Professional journalists, caught in the battle, see their autonomy and independence increasingly threatened, as happened in Russia after the dissolution of the Soviet Union. Where state-run broadcast networks dominate the market and economic constraints limit the entry of many new nonstate broadcasters, conditions for neutral and objective reporting become strained. Then, only a powerful buffer organization can protect the economic and personnel stability of a free broadcast press.

*The legal system* in many countries can furnish a means for seeking better balance in broadcasting, but very often there is no provision in the broadcast law for requesting a court decision on alleged violations: imbalance, misrepresentation, lack of representation, and other problems raised earlier. Instead, citizens will have to request hearings under general statutes, which may turn out to be inadequate for cases involving broadcasting. U.S. broadcast law, particularly in the form of FCC rules and regulations, is quite specific, and all cases decided by the FCC can be appealed through the court system. Canada operates in a roughly similar manner, but few other countries do. In part, that may be due to a general feeling on the part of the public that appealing through the courts will do little good. But it also may be the case that the abundance of lawyers, including specialists in communications law, helps to encourage Americans to use the legal system, whereas such lawyers are far less common, if they exist at all, in other countries. And if broadcasting functions as a government monopoly, complainants must realize that they are contending with the government itself.

Ethnic minorities in particular may feel that they have little hope of success if they must work through the majority culture's legal system, especially if their own conception of what is legal is quite different. For example, many Southeast Asian communities that have taken root in the United States since the end of the Vietnam War, e.g., Hmong, have had problems within the U.S. legal system over their rights to observe traditional customs. Issues such as treatment of wives and appropriate ages for marriage have placed mainstream culture and various Southeast Asian cultures in conflict on several occasions. In most cases, U.S. courts have had little sympathy for the view that "traditional" cultural practices should prevail, and mainstream media accounts of such cases rarely indicate the nature and basis of "traditional" viewpoints. An individual arguing that her or his views were being excluded by the media probably could not count on much support from the courts.

*Quangos* (quasi-nongovernmental organizations) have developed in a few countries as yet another line of approach in the regulation of the electronic media. These usually take the specific form of councils, financed through annual budgetary appropriations and carrying some of the authority of government through the laws that establish them. However, they usually are not staffed by civil service, nor are they often a part of the table of organization of any government ministry. Their supervisory boards are likely to be made up of a wide range of the citizenry— business people, religious authorities, retirees, ethnic minorities—who themselves are appointed by the legislative body. They may have limited power to penalize offenders, or they may be advisory; but they usually file annual reports of their activities, and may release reports of specific findings, as well.

Great Britain has two such councils: the Broadcasting Complaints Commission (1981) and the Broadcasting Standards Council (1988). The former limits itself to consideration of individual complaints of unfair or unjust treatment, or invasion of privacy, through a broadcast program. The latter has a much broader mandate: to consider the portrayal of violence, sex, taste, and decency in programming, British-made or imported. It has developed, and regularly revises, a code of practice which spells out acceptable standards, themselves derived from interviews of broadcasters, religious authorities, educators, and members of the general public. (The Council holds numerous public meetings throughout Britain each year.) In cases involving specific complaints about programs, both bodies may require broadcasters to publicize their findings, through broadcasting and/or through print.

Regarding ethnic minorities, the BSC Code states, *inter alia,* "Use of derogatory terms in speaking of men and women of other races and nations almost invariably gives offense and should be avoided where the context does not warrant it. . . . The presentation of minority groups as an undifferentiated mass, rather than a collection of individuals with limited interests in common, should be discouraged." One provision among many regarding the portrayal of conflict—which in this Code almost always means *violent* conflict—reads as follows: "Where scenes of violence are necessarily included in television bulletins, the fact that violence has bloody consequences should not be glossed over. However, it is not for the broadcaster to impose a moral judgment on the audience and care should be taken not to linger on the casualties nor on the bloody evidence of violence."

How much impact either of these two bodies has on programming practices is debatable. Both have attempted to reach decisions in a balanced manner, taking into account the contentions of both broadcasters and complainants. Neither seems to have been influenced in any major respect by the ruling (since 1979) Conservative Party, although there were many expressions of fear on the part of broadcasters and others that the Council in particular was created expressly for the purpose of further imposing Thatcherite control over broadcasting; nor does either appear to have been intimidated by the broadcasters. The Council has gone to far greater effort than has the Commission to travel around the country seeking public input, and its research studies, on the portrayal of violence, ethnic minorities, and other elements of society, have won praise from scholars and at least some of the "media community."

Growing public concern over the portrayal of violence on television has led several countries, most of them in the English-speaking world, to consider the creation of similar quangos. If they proceed, they should bear in mind that Great Britain's two quangos were established and staffed in such a way that political and media interference with them would be difficult; that the Council in particular spends a great deal of time interacting with the public, which seems to have increased public awareness and respect for its work; that both bodies can *require* broadcast coverage of their recommendations; and that both have worked *with* broadcasters, rather than against them, to help broadcasting make its contribution to a healthy society. The Council does seem to have adopted an overly narrow approach to the portrayal of conflict by defining it almost exclusively in terms of violence; and the Commission has done little to make itself more "user friendly" to the public in general, let alone the ethnic minority public, which is likely to be skeptical as to the use of such a body to seek fairer and more accurate portrayal through broadcasting. If a nation is able to take all of that into account when designing a quango, there may be some quite beneficial results.

*Citizens' groups,* finally, have assembled at one time or another to bring pressure to bear on broadcasting for its handling of ethnic minority programming and hiring, and for its coverage of conflict. Such bodies really are not regulatory, in that they have no power to require broadcasters to do as the bodies wish, but they can be visible and credible enough to attract wider public and media attention, and thus to bring broadcasters to treat those wishes seriously.

Some citizens' groups disappear once a particular crisis ends or its members lose interest or energy, while others fade away gradually. Still others have remained in existence for 10, 20, 30, even more than 50 years. Most of the longer-lived groups seem to have been single-issue centered: television's influence on children; the moral character of television fiction; sex on TV; fairness and ac-curacy in news and public affairs; portrayal and hiring of ethnic

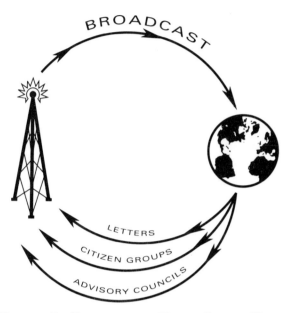

## *Audience Influence on Broadcast Content*

minorities and/or women; etc. Those groups also seem to have been successful in raising operating funds, perhaps because people often will give to specific causes which they favor, but not to general approaches which might sometimes include their favorite causes.

In the United States in the 1960s, the Office of Communication of the United Church of Christ (UCC) turned its attention from religious broadcasting to the failure of local broadcasters to give adequate attention to minority groups within their service areas. UCC combined with local citizens groups to confront a particularly one-sided, segregationist broadcaster in Jackson, Mississippi, and eventually to challenge its license before the Federal Communications Commission. The case led not only to the principle that viewers had the right to participate in license renewal hearings before the FCC, but also to the loss of that broadcaster's license.

As a result, many citizens groups have challenged license renewals in the United States for broadcasters' shortcomings in meeting the needs and interests of minorities and women in their service areas, and for failing to hire sufficient numbers of minorities in management positions at the stations. Organizations such as the National Black Media Coalition and the National Latino Media Coalition have tried to enforce equal employment laws to the letter, and have gained a certain amount of success. Even though the broadcaster obtains renewal in over 99 percent of the cases, often a broadcaster will improve its record as a result of, or to resist, such a challenge.

Great Britain's National Viewers and Listeners Association (VALA) was developed by a school headmistress, Mary Whitehouse, in 1964. She was concerned over rising levels of teenage pregnancy and violence, and sought to bring pressure to bear on broadcasters to reduce levels of violence and of sexual display, particularly on television. She attempted at first to deal directly with broadcasters, but found her bargaining power increasing as the print media began to provide coverage of her disagreements with the BBC and Independent Broadcasting Authority. That also helped to publicize her association, and, together with her books on the subject, increased the Association's membership to something over 10,000. Prime Minister Thatcher championed her cause, and appeared with her in public. Broadcasters were not willing to concede that her efforts led to what at least some critics regarded as a decrease in sexual display on television; nor was the Broadcasting Standards Council comfortable with the notion that she was, in certain respects, its "godmother." She probably deserves some credit for both.

UCC and VALA illustrate several aspects of successful citizen group involvement in broadcasting. Broadcasters cannot blithely ignore such groups in the hope or expectation that they will fade away. Some of them do, but those which are well organized, feature dynamic leadership, and work on "hot" topics where society is concerned, probably will attract print media attention, where the broadcasters are apt to be presented as arrogant or out of touch with society. If the group wins the attention of political, and perhaps religious, leaders, it will be difficult to dismiss lightly, whether it is seen as *vox populi* or not.

Certain ethnic groups have been organized to deal with television portrayals, hiring practices, and the work of broadcast regulatory agencies. The National Black Media Coalition and *La Raza* (Hispanic-American) in the United States; the Campaign Against Racism in the Media and Black Media Workers' Association in Great Britain; Te Reo Irirangi Maori in New Zealand—all are examples of groups that have worked to improve the depiction of ethnic minorities through such channels as the legal recognition of a Maori right to broadcast frequencies; nomination of the first African-American Commissioner to serve on the U.S. FCC; and the making of a 30-minute film for TV, which was shown on the BBC's *Open Door* (access) program, and which dealt with racist images conveyed through BBC drama, comedy, and news programs.

Perhaps the tiniest of ethnic groups to seek improved portrayal through broadcasting is the Ainu, the original inhabitants of Japan. There may be some thousands, or even tens of thousands, of people with Ainu blood, but only a few hundred speak the language, and perhaps 10 or 20 with some fluency. Should the Kurile Islands be returned to Japan by Russia, an Ainu association is campaigning to be allowed to settle them and to establish a broadcasting service which would serve as one instrument for the revival of the Ainu language. The association already is making videotapes in Ainu, which raises an interesting point: the demands of some groups for electronic media exposure, under certain conditions, might be met more satisfactorily through nonbroadcast channels, such as duplication and distribution of audio- and videotape cassettes. The cost and the efficiency of cassettes may be far better than broadcasting when certain delimited aims and audiences are involved. But those technologies lack the symbolic value of broadcast outlets.

There also are cases where citizens' groups with seemingly important and societally attractive aims have not met with success, despite persistence and careful organization. Japan's commercial television networks, which perhaps show more and uglier violence (and thus conflict) than do any other broadcasters anywhere else, have come under attack by various citizens groups, most of them organized by angry parents and schoolteachers. They have had little effect on the reduction of either the amount or the nature of TV violence. The Japanese commercial networks are owned by the major Japanese newspapers, and both are linked closely with "establishment" politicians in a symbiotic relationship where the media generally avoid calling attention to politicians' shortcomings, while the politicians avoid passage of any bills that might increase the currently low level of government regulation of broadcast programming.

\*　\*　\*　\*　\*

The many forms of regulatory, quasi-regulatory, and group influence presented here all seem to lead to one general conclusion: If such a body, governmental or otherwise, is supported by those holding real political or economic power, and if that body is headed by someone with persistence, independence of thought and action, and a reasonably solid knowledge of the electronic media, then there might be some hope that regulation could help those media to play a more significant role in shaping a fairer, more open, more peaceful society. Weak regulatory bodies only increase the cynicism of ethnic minorities, and of those working to reduce conflict, regarding any meaningful reform.

The existence of such bodies also acts as a challenge to the notion of media autonomy, of course. Perhaps the best perspective for the media to take is to consider the efforts of citizens' groups, quangos, and others as sincere attempts to help. Such a perspective could dispel much of the hostility that seems to arise among media staff and group members alike when such groups first appear on the scene. If staff make it clear that they consider themselves responsible in the final analysis for what they present to the public, but are willing to listen and sometimes act on what groups tell them, both sides will come out ahead, and even may stop thinking of themselves as separate sides. If offers of help turn out not to be sincere, at least the media can say that they've tried.

# CITIZENS' GROUPS AS BROADCASTERS

As we have seen, certain citizens' groups have worked through various regulatory and quasiregulatory bodies to bring about change in ethnic minority portrayals and employment in the electronic media. While few of them have expressed the desire to operate their own services, they have helped to establish an overall climate in which ethnic minority groups have found such a possibility increasingly common.

Expatriate communities of ethnic minorities in several large European cities—Paris (North African Arabs), Amsterdam (South Moluccans and Surinamese), Cologne-Dusseldorf-Essen (Yugoslavs)—have organized themselves to combat media stereotyping in their respective locales by protesting existing portrayals, but also by creating their own programming. The Yugoslav groups appear to have had only modest success. However, the Arabs in Paris, and in a few other large cities in France, did succeed in obtaining radio licenses from the French regulatory agencies. The Surinamese and Moluccans, as well as some other ethnic minorities living in the Netherlands, have secured ongoing financial support from the Dutch Ministry of Culture for making television programs about themselves. These are shown through the *migranttelevisie* service, which appears largely on cable TV (widespread in the Netherlands).

Australia has a Special Broadcasting Service, which offers radio and TV programming in original languages from many Asian, Middle Eastern, and European broadcast services; and over 20 Aboriginal-operated media services, including Imparja Television (Alice Springs). New Zealand has licensed roughly two dozen local radio stations operated by Maori, and finances a national Maori news service, Mana Maori Media. The New Zealand Broadcasting Corporation's Access Radio service also provides airtime for ethnic and linguistic minorities. Citizens' groups had a great deal to do with the creation of Maori and Aboriginal broadcasting, chiefly through pressure applied on members of parliament (there are a few Aboriginal and Maori M.P.s, as well, who were of some help) and on the Department of Aboriginal Affairs and the Ministry of Maori Affairs. They had little to do with the establishment of New Zealand's Access Radio or Australia's SBS.

Third World nations feature rather little citizen group activity of any sort. Many of those countries have autocratic governments which operate the often monopoly-structured broadcast services (still common in Africa and in Asia) in their own interests, which may or may not coincide with the interests of minorities. However, most of them will provide services in several of the dozens or even hundreds of languages spoken in the country. India's All-India Radio (AIR) and Doordarshan (TV) are controlled by the Hindu-led Congress Party. Hindi predominates, but AIR offers programs in 19 languages and Doordarshan in perhaps six. Local television has been slow to develop—only four Indian cities have a separate channel for it—but local radio is spreading quite rapidly, and caters primarily to the dominant ethnic and linguistic groups in each region it serves. That approach may help to lessen interethnic tension, but it works well only so long as broadcasting remains a monopoly. India's monopoly already was breached

106

in a modest way when local commercial TV services began to be licensed in 1991, although those services provide little but entertainment.

Doordarshan now faces a far more serious challenge, as tens of millions of Indians in cities and rural areas acquire the capability to receive TV signals directly from satellites. Viewers so equipped (or with neighbors so equipped) could watch CNN and BBC World TV (Asia) coverage of Muslim and Hindu clashes in Bombay and elsewhere in 1992 and 1993, whereas Doordarshan provided abbreviated, "sanitized" accounts of the fighting. Indian authorities were disturbed over the possibility that CNN and BBC coverage could lead to still more interethnic fighting, although there is no indication that it did. Nor has it yet led to the formation of citizens' groups seeking change in AIR or Doordarshan policies. However, that example underscores the difficulties faced by governments wishing to block public access to other broadcast versions, some from outside the country, of domestic events. To add to the problem, political, religious, and other groups are now preparing and distributing videocassette "magazines" which include coverage of political and other situations and crises unlikely to be seen over Doordarshan.

In Latin America, native American (Amerindian) groups have gone largely unnoticed by the mainstream (Spanish-language) media. Recently, however, several religious organizations—mainly Catholic, but Baha'i and Seventh Day Adventist, as well—have been working with such groups to get them interested in making broadcasts for themselves, and in their own languages. Their efforts often have borne fruit: Training programs have helped to develop qualified production staff. However, some of those staff members have come to feel sufficiently independent to challenge what they sometimes regard as an overly narrow religious character to the programming, which may not have been the outcome the religious organization would have predicted or desired! A few have become station managers, even though the training programs generally have not offered specific training in the area of management.

There have been similar efforts in Africa, but Latin America has proven to be more fertile ground: Most African nations still consider broadcasting as a monopoly of the state, while most Latin American nations license many broadcast outlets (more than two dozen radio stations in Quito, Ecuador). Still, Burkina Faso and Senegal have had interesting experiments involving the basic question, How do you bring people who have been neglected by radio, and may doubt that it can help them, to try it out? How can you get them to wish to become involved with radio, or any other mass medium?

In Burkina Faso, a few broadcasters from the African Center for Rural Radio Studies in Ouagadougou (the capital) held a "radio day" in the town of Toudou. The broadcasters, once they had become somewhat familiar with the local situation, played the role of government officials, and the villagers expressed their complaints. The broadcasters taped the complaints, brought them back to the capital, and recorded the responses that actual government officials made to them. They then returned to the village and played the responses over a loudspeaker set up for the occasion. In this way, the broadcasters hoped, villagers might gain confidence that radio could be of real benefit to them. Once that happened, the broadcasters could actually have some hope of producing a regularly scheduled rural radio program that would be a true reflection of people's goals and frustrations. Unfortunately, a *coup d'état* took place soon thereafter (October 1987) and the new government closed the Center.

Senegal carried out a similar experiment, but over a longer period of time. Radio Educative Rurale, which operates within Senegal's national (monopoly) broadcast service, initiated a program series entitled "Dissoo" (Wolof for "understanding and dialogue") in 1968. UNESCO paid most of the costs for it in its pilot project stage, but ceased to fund it after 1974, at which time the Senegalese government assumed financial responsibility for it. Broadcast staff, generally chosen for their understanding of, and empathy with, rural dwellers and their situations, went out into the countryside. They elicited and recorded the opinions of villagers regarding the problems they faced, but especially problems with which the government might be expected to help. The broadcasters then recorded responses from government officials to the villagers, and the combined material was broadcast. At first, government officials were uncooperative, in part because the various linguistic minority rural populations had no political clout, but Senegalese President Senghor backed the program, and cooperation improved. Eventually, the president turned his attention more heavily to other matters, money to support broadcaster trips to rural areas dried up, and "Dissoo," still on the air today, became a shadow of its former self.

\* \* \* \* \*

The experiences of citizens' groups with the electronic media vary a good deal, but have certain elements in common: Many groups have perceived broadcasting as having real utility for them only after they have seen specific results coming from programs they have made or in which they were directly involved. Once they have decided to seek authorization to broadcast, they have found the process difficult, and often have relied on the help of certain powerful individuals or agencies to obtain that authorization. In some cases, those individuals or agencies may have been disappointed to see the groups reduce or drop certain types of programming, but one must assume that such groups, once they're actually on the air, will want to discover their own broadcast voices and follow their own agendas. Finally, money to support such group activities generally is in short supply, although, as we shall see, there are a few reasonably well-financed endeavors in existence which show that it *is* possible to find the means, if the will is there.

# WHO WILL PAY,
# AND AT WHAT COST?

If the electronic media are to improve their coverage of conflict and ethnic minorities, there will be some major costs in the form of added staff, expanded archives, larger travel expenses, and other items. It seems fair enough that the media organizations themselves bear those added costs. The media do receive certain privileges as licensees, including what usually amounts to the continuing right to hold them. Certainly there are stations which have lost their licenses in some countries—France, Canada, Great Britain, the United States, Chile, Nicaragua—but such instances make up a tiny fraction of the whole. Furthermore, the electronic media should consider it to be in their own best interests to improve their coverage of conflict and ethnic minorities, if only because that is a tangible display of good citizenship. And it can be good business—adding audiences to the station.

However, improving coverage of ethnic minorities may involve some very specific costs that will be considerably greater than the electronic media alone should be expected to bear. That is quite likely when the ethnic minority population is sizable and if the overall record of its neglect is of long duration. The media might be expected to cover at least some of the costs for training programs, and to advise and assist separate ethnic minority stations, as many of them already do. But there will be large additional costs for training if it must include housing and feeding trainees. Also, if there are to be separate stations for ethnic minorities, as well as better access and more equitable treatment through mainstream media, there will be the considerable costs of building and maintaining such services.

New Zealand sets aside at least 6 percent (but it usually comes to 10 percent or more) of each year's general income from annual license fees for the specific support of Maori radio and television. That is justified in part on the grounds that Maori make up at least 6 percent of the national population. Nations without license fee-based systems could consider alternatives such as surtaxes on existing broadcast stations, or on the sales prices of radio and TV sets, although neither one will be popular with those who have to pay. However, special funding quotas from whatever source, if they are based upon percentages of population, are bound to leave out some minorities and underrepresent others, if only because census data usually underreport ethnic minorities.

Governments, whether national, regional, or local, can play a role in financing a portion of such expanded activity. If a minority is distributed over an entire nation, then the national government should play a major, and possibly leading, role in funding that activity. Several governments do so, in a variety of ways. As already noted, Sweden, Norway, and Denmark have furnished the transmitters for the *närradio* services, and have subsidized the studio-to-transmitter links. France provides annual subsidies to nonprofit, noncommercial radio stations, a number of which are operated by and for ethnic minorities. Canada subsidized Native American radio stations until 1990; the United States provided start-up funding for Native American radio stations during the 1970s. Australia's government-supported Special Broadcasting Service provides separate chan-

112

nels of radio and television programming in a multitude of languages, including Greek, Dutch, and Indonesian.

Canada, Australia, New Zealand, and several other countries sometimes have funded summer internships or even year-round entry-level jobs for ethnic minorities, some of whom have worked for media operations. The Australian government's Department of Employment Education and Training provided wage support for Aboriginal trainees in the Australian Broadcasting Corporation, but there had to be a guarantee of employment following successful completion of training. Thanks to that assistance, the numbers of Aboriginal staff in ABC's Radio Division rose from two in 1985 to 30 in early 1991.

Regional and local governments are less likely to help support electronic media in any form, whether for minorities or not. However, certain of the Canadian provincial governments (Quebec, Ontario) have subsidized native American radio stations, and Alaska has done likewise for Inuit and Native American stations there. The former German Democratic Republic supported a several-hour-per-day radio service in Sorbish, a Slavic language spoken by perhaps 20,000 people living in the southeast corner of the state of Saxony. With the advent of German unification in 1991, broadcasting in the former GDR became the responsibility of each state, and the Sorb service became the joint responsibility of the states involved with the two broadcast operations (Mitteldeutscher Rundfunk and Ostdeutscher Rundfunk Brandenburg) serving the area. The city of Toronto helps to support a multilingual (chiefly European languages) radio station there.

Broadcasting organizations themselves often provide funding for similar purposes. The state public service operations in Norway, Sweden, and Finland all support the full costs of Sami ("Lapp") radio services, drawing from the annual license fee income to do so. Ireland's Raidio Telefis

113

Eirann does likewise for the Irish (Gaelic) language service, Raidio na Gaeltachta, and for Gaelic television programming broadcast through RTE. The BBC uses a portion of its license fee revenue to fund BBC Radio Cymru (Welsh) and Raidio nan Gaidheal (Scots Gaelic). All India Radio supports more than 40 local radio stations, most of them broadcasting in local languages, through its annual government appropriation. Brazil's national radio service, RadioBras, serves some of the Amazon basin's Amerindian population in their own languages through its Radio Nacional da Amazonia, again with funding through annual government appropriation.

Broadcasters in the United States, Canada, Australia, New Zealand, and elsewhere sometimes have donated used equipment to ethnic minority stations; certain of those coun-tries have tax incentives which encourage such donations. Great Britain's Channel Four, a commercial TV service, has financed the production of a number of films, including some dealing with minority-majority culture relationships (e.g., *My Beautiful Launderette,* which portrayed the business aspirations of a young south Asian man living in London). It has assessed the potential profitability of each such venture very carefully, and often has earned a profit through a combination of cinema and television exhibition of the films.

Certain societal institutions, chiefly religious organizations and nonprofit foundations, have made important financial and advisory contributions to the development of ethnic minority stations (usually radio) and programs. The Catholic Church, sometimes at the local level, sometimes national, occasionally international, has financed and advised stations for various Amerindian communities in Latin America. Radio "Voice of the Coast," founded in Osorno, Chile in 1968, originally was intended to educate the Mapuche living in the area. It seems to have had some effect in the form of increased literacy, but it also serves as an important source of daily news for its listeners, and reinforces and "validates" the Mapuche language itself.

Ethnic minority groups themselves, although they often are among the most impoverished members of society, some-times have provided stations with financial support. Certain of the Maori tribes in New Zealand have furnished buildings, money for equipment, and partial salaries of certain individuals, often administrators. Native American tribes and bands in North America, such as the Navajo and Ojibwa (Anishinabe), have done likewise, sometimes with the help of money earned through business enterprises, such as mining, gambling casinos, fishing, and building construction. However, some of them expect the stations to become income-producers over time, mainly through sale of advertising time and through radio bingo games. The latter is especially common among Native American radio stations in Canada, and is somewhat controversial, in that it might encourage gambling among individuals who have little disposable income, but who are tempted, against the odds, to "strike it rich."

Commercial advertising and sponsorship sometimes draw criticism because they may influence ethnic minority stations to become more mainstream in their programming, so as to be more attractive to advertisers. However, that need not be a negative influence: Advertisers should have every reason to support stations which attempt to better the lot of their audiences. If the stations are successful, advertisers will have increased numbers of more prosperous customers. Therefore, it could pay an advertiser to support an ethnic minority station, or ethnic minority programming on a mainstream station. A few sponsors have helped meet the costs of certain U.S. public television series and single programs about the experiences of ethnic minorities, such as the highly acclaimed series about the

African-American struggle for civil rights, *Eyes on the Prize*. The U.S. Public Broadcasting Service itself made money available for that and other programs, through a special fund for the support of ethnic minority, experimental, and other sorts of nonmainstream programming. (PBS receives much of its funding through annual governmental appropriations.) However, neither sponsor nor PBS support began to meet the cost of producing *Eyes on the Prize*. Its producer gathered the remaining funds from personal friends and various institutions.

*   *   *   *   *

There are still other, if perhaps less significant, sources of financial support for ethnic minority broadcasting, but the list above should indicate two things: First, that there are many potential sources; and second, that no single source is likely to suffice. Even when a single source is found, that generosity may last only so long as the economy is healthy. With economic downturn may come pressures to cut back on government or individual broadcast service expenditures; unless ethnic minority groups have considerable political clout, they are apt to find themselves with reduced or no funding. Canadian federal government funding of Native American stations was eliminated in 1990 because of Canada's recession; the Sami Radio service within Sweden's Sveriges Radio suffered budget cuts in 1993 due to a combination of tighter budgets and changing priorities at SR.

Therefore, ethnic minority broadcasters must be prepared to spend considerable time lobbying on their own behalves, as well as patching together support from most or all types of financial sources. Many U.S. public broadcasters employ one or more full-time fund raisers for just that reason, but the investment in such staff can pay handsome dividends. Ethnic minority stations might consider following suit.

# LANGUAGES
# AND PERCEPTIONS

Even in the best of all worlds, where money to support expanded ethnic minority broadcasting and coverage of conflict is plentiful, there remains the question of how to go about the reshaping of the electronic media so that they will play more meaningful roles in the creation of more tolerant, peaceful, healthy societies. We have suggested several structural ways of going about the task: councils, training schemes, approaches to information gathering, role-playing, etc. But there remains the most vital step of all: how to depict, through words and visual images, what a healthy society should be.

As we have indicated, it is very difficult to sustain the argument that NOT displaying conflict and intolerance is the best way to meet the goal. Experiences in China, India, the former Soviet Union, and many other places show that such a strategy may keep interethnic tensions under wraps, but it doesn't appear to diminish them. And where there was a seemingly airtight monopoly over the airwaves, people's fertile minds often created elaborate scenarios out of scraps of rumor, and these may have been far worse than the reality of a given situation. Also, individuals whose everyday experiences contain the usual human mixture of good and bad are unlikely to believe everything they hear and see over a media system which portrays only the positive aspects of national life. That simply is too far removed from the reality of those everyday experiences.

Assume, then, that the electronic media will deal with the realities of a society—"warts and all," as Oliver Cromwell allegedly told his portrait painter. How should they do so in order to be most effective? It sounds simplistic to observe that, while much depends upon just what the media choose to tell and show, and how thoroughly and evenhandedly they choose to cover events, at least as much depends upon *how:* the specific words and phrases chosen, the specific visual images accompanying or dominating those words and phrases.

The "how" of electronic communication is a vast subject, and a vast amount has been written about it. Furthermore, various studies conducted over time and in many different cultures make it clear that people communicate in a wide variety of ways, which means that they also have many different ways of interpreting what they see and hear. If one picture is worth a thousand words (highly doubtful), they certainly would not be the same words to all people. That is true not only across national borders, but also within nations. What is more, situations involving conflict and tension appear to exaggerate differences in interpretation, as individuals are even more likely to perceive what they want to perceive.

If there is a valid universal observation on the complex subject of words and images, it is this: Electronic media personnel involved with program production and decision-making have the obligation to be especially sensitive to the fact that interpretations of words and images will vary within and between cultures. Increasingly, people around the world receive their first news of events through the electronic media. That alone imposes a special responsibility on media staff. But research on the linkage between televised violence and violence in real life indicates quite

118

clearly that television does play a role, and perhaps an important role, in shaping people's attitudes toward violence; and that is still further reason for staff responsibility in any treatment of conflict.

It is quite true that differences in interpretations of words and images often will be slight enough that media staff need not worry about them. It is also true that variation in interpretations can be exceptionally difficult to detect, although it may emerge more clearly if stations turn to their ethnic minority staff and to the resource persons they have identified in ethnic minority communities, universities, etc., for advice. If use of those resources still leaves media staff in doubt over whether to use certain words or phrases or to show certain visual images, and if there is considerable tension within society at the moment, it would seem wiser to simply avoid using a term or image that could be taken as slighting, demeaning, racist, or even overly stereotypical. Many broadcast newsrooms have developed detailed guidelines for the use or nonuse of such terms as *terrorist, black, yellow,* etc. All newsrooms should have them, and update them regularly, as the BBC and numerous others have done.

Such guidelines should be developed in light of everyday language use, rather than dictionary definitions of terms. That is particularly important when dealing with emotional situations, where ethnic minorities may apropriate majority culture terms and use them in very different ways. The term "bad" began to be used by African-Americans some years ago to indicate something that commanded respect, rather than something negative. But if a majority culture journalist were to use that term to describe an African-American, there almost certainly would be confusion over the intended meaning.

Nonverbal messages often resist stable definition, as well. A close-up shot of an individual often serves to underline a visual statement. Show a close-up of an identifiable ethnic minority youth at a disturbance of some sort, with eyes blazing, and the likely majority culture reaction will be, "There's another one of those out-of-control ******s who thinks she/he can get away with anything." That might be true, but the eyes also might be blazing because the individual's house has just been burned to the ground by other individuals of the same or another ethnic minority, or the majority. Accompanying audio material might explain that, but often such images are allowed to "speak" for themselves, even if what they "say" isn't what the individual means. If the images are graphic enough, the reporter's words, if any, can easily be ignored, especially when the images reinforce existing visual stereotypes.

That raises yet another important point about the languages of the electronic media. Not only do certain recurring visual and aural images tend to reinforce stereotypes—whoever holds them, whether accurate or not (and "accurate" to whom?)—but they also may lose their impact (shock value) with frequent repetition, especially if used often within a brief period of time. U.S. TV coverage of starvation in Somalia may have helped to awaken the U.S. public to the nature of the disaster, as well as to the conflict that had caused it, but there were periods when virtually every report about the country showed at least some images of starving individuals, usually children and often in fly-covered close-up shots. Similarly, television coverage of the aftermath of the Los Angeles "riots" in April 1992 concentrated heavily on block after block of burned-out buildings. It was not unusual to hear viewers state, after no more than a week or two of such coverage, "I wish they'd show something else. Those pictures are so boring/sickening/upsetting/repetitious [the list could go on] that I'm tired of seeing them." Such perceptions often appear to be linked to viewer's feelings that TV tends to exaggerate, especially in visual terms.

The same perception also may apply to verbal terms. An April 1993, bombing carried out by the IRA in London was the subject of many call-in programs. A number of individuals specifically stated that they thought the media exaggerated the effectiveness of the bombings, and, in so doing, led the IRA to think that they continued to be useful. Furthermore, said some of the callers, the very language used in media reports on the bombings *is* at times exaggerated; several referred to a report in one of the more sensationalist British newspapers which said that the bombing had "brought London to a screeching halt." The phrase may have been colorful, but the reality was that most Londoners and visitors were unaffected by the blast, and unaware of it until it had been reported.

There is a final note of caution about uses of language in situations of tension and conflict where ethnic minorities are involved. If one of the sides has a markedly different cultural background, and especially if its members speak a markedly different language, then reporters, editors, and managers should be especially careful to attempt to understand exactly what those individuals are saying. Some will misuse what may be their second language (the language of the majority culture) and, as a result, may employ terms that are far more, or less, hostile or conciliatory than what they really want to express. Some may be showing their very deepest feelings when they speak softly, while others may do so by shouting. Some may avert their eyes as a sign of respect, confusion, or shyness (especially if they're not accustomed to being recorded), while others may look aside out of hatred or for concealment.

If electronic media personnel had to consider every nuance of every verbal and nonverbal expression made in the course of a conflict or at times of interracial tension, then producing the news or entertainment would be a very slow process—and the electronic media, whatever else they may be, are not slow to report, or even to dramatize.

Technology helps to make instant, or nearly instant, production easier than ever. However, it is up to human beings to be sensitive enough to variant uses and interpretations of words and images, especially when connected with conflict and tension in a multiethnic society; to know when to slow down the production process so that they might question old habits and stereotypes; and then to get the stories they are relating, whether fact or fiction, as "right" as possible for the promotion of a healthier society.

# AN AFTERWORD, OR,
# ON TO THE 21ST CENTURY

Many of the problems that arise in television's coverage of ethnic minorities, especially in situations involving conflict, are common to TV news in general. Television's emphasis on stories with powerful visual content often distorts the image of ethnic minorities in society by featuring them in "colorful" protest marches, demonstrations, and confrontations with government and law enforcement officials. Other minorities, whether activists in pro- or anti-abortion groups, defenders of animal rights, protesters against nuclear energy, or any of a variety of other collections of people seeking change, are presented to the larger society through television in many of the same images. The brevity of TV newscast items in most broadcast systems means that such groups often are portrayed through their most angry, sensational, or provocative statements, to the accompaniment of clenched fists, bared teeth, or staring eyes. If TV news is to change the way in which it portrays ethnic minorities, it will have to alter its coverage of minorities of all sorts.

Documentaries offer the opportunity for in-depth coverage, and thus, the prospect of more balanced, thorough treatment of ethnic and other minorities. However, television documentaries are becoming something of an endangered species in many countries, for two major reasons. First, they are expensive. As more and more countries add commercial TV alongside their former public service monopoly systems, audiences become less enthusiastic about the prospect of having their annual license fees, or annual government appropriations, increased to support the public system. Assuming that there will be some degree of inflation, that will mean less money for the public system over time. Program production is almost certain to suffer as a result. Second, documentaries are favorite targets for criticism on the part of government officials, who sometimes threaten to cut appropriations because of them; newspapers, which often seem to take pleasure in reporting the alleged inadequacies of a rival medium of communication; special interest groups, whether religious, economic, educational, or ethnic minority; and a number of others. Therefore, not only are they costly to make, but they can be costly to defend, especially if they lead to lawsuits, license challenges, or budget cuts.

When money is scarce, broadcasters usually become very cost-conscious. Very often, the first programs to suffer are those which attract the smallest audiences, along with those which attract the most criticism. Documentaries usually do not attract many viewers, especially if they deal with controversial issues. (Nature documentaries, in contrast, are quite popular.) If public service broadcasters face budget cuts as well as pressures on license fee or government appropriations support, they are not likely to reduce spending on popular programs, particularly if the public, but also government officials, would feel that such reductions were being made in order to maintain the present level of documentary production.

Commercial broadcasters use much the same reasoning, in the sense that high-cost programs which don't attract large audiences are bad for the budgetary health of a station or network. Because commercial broadcasters are licensed by the government, and receive considerable attention from the press, they, too, will be careful not to offend too many interests, in part because the advertisers which support commercial stations usually don't care to be associated with controversial matters.

As we move toward the 21st century, and an era of increasing "channel abundance" for audiences throughout most of the industrialized world, the pressures just noted are likely to become even more severe. Audiences wishing to avoid provocative or controversial programs that make them feel uneasy, guilty, or simply uninformed will find it much easier to do so when there are plenty of other choices available through TV. That will make it even more difficult for documentary producers to justify their high costs. It will take real courage of conviction on the part of station managers to support such programs, or even newscasts which seem too depressing, controversial, or inconclusive. (Many viewers seem to prefer newscasts that wrap things up neatly.)

That may be an overly gloomy prediction, but in country after country where channel choice has increased, and especially where commercial TV has been added to the system, there has been an increase in the amount of viewing of non-informational or pseudo-informational ("reality-based" programs such as *Rescue: 911,* "docudramas," etc.) programming. That increase usually hasn't been accompanied by a decrease in the viewing of TV newscasts, but there is some evidence that the newscasts themselves may be increasing the amounts of "good news" coverage, and that readers and anchorpersons may be exhibiting more "user-friendly" styles of presentation. That does not bode well for the in-depth, balanced, serious treatment of conflict in society that is so sorely needed.

But there are ways to overcome the viewer-avoidance problems just noted, assuming that stations and networks continue to feel that they have an obligation to present conflict in ways that will truly help lead to fair and lasting resolutions, and also to present society with balanced images of ethnic minority life. First, they should increase their involvement with educational institutions at all levels, but especially with the primary grades. If documentaries and even, on occasion, newscast items, were made readily and easily available to schools (admittedly not a simple task, if talent royalties, copyright issues, etc., are involved), that could help to educate new generations in two ways: increased understanding of conflict, and tolerance for diversity, in society; and greater appreciation of the role of television in providing such material.

Most primary school systems offer courses that deal with the nature of society, whether domestic, foreign, or both. Documentaries on conflict and ethnic minority experiences can be splendid visual illustrations of such situations. Furthermore, they may even benefit from not having been made for classroom use, since they aren't likely to seem to talk down to students. Teachers can explain the more difficult concepts, and, if videocassette copies are readily available, can review specific segments. Video compact disks, as they become more plentiful and economical, will make it even easier to retrieve segments. Also, the public and governments should appreciate the broadcaster's sense of economy in such reuse of program material.

Broadcast officials might even consider working with teachers to develop greater media literacy on the part of students, so that students, and perhaps teachers as well, would have a better understanding of the selective nature of television coverage. In the process, they also might learn to distinguish more readily between material that was recorded on-site, recreated, "suggested by" other events ("this is what *might* have happened), or fabricated on the basis of no evidence whatsoever. That is asking a great deal of broadcasters, since TV and the other mass media do not

126

take readily to self-criticism. However, public service broad-casters in France, Great Britain, Germany, the United States, and the former Soviet Union at one time or another have held open, televised forums with viewers in which people were invited to express their feelings about various aspects of television. If one considers the situation in purely competitive terms, a station or network which exercises such self-criticism and works with school children to "demystify" the medium would probably stand a good chance of retaining their loyalty as they become adult viewers.

Second, broadcasters with a real commitment to the serious coverage of conflict and ethnic minority affairs will have to increase their promotion of such coverage, whether through on-air announcements of forthcoming programs, purchase of print media space for program publicity, mass mailings to special-interest groups (computer-generated lists of members of organizations are becoming increasingly common, although such lists are expensive), announce-ments to schools as part of the media literacy effort noted just above, or in the course of personal contact with the audience, perhaps during group visits to stations, at which time attendees could be given promotional brochures on the station's forthcoming documentaries. The increasing avail-ability of videotext services in cable systems offers yet another prospective channel for reaching potentially inter-ested viewers.

A third approach is worth considering, even if it may be time consuming and relatively expensive. It is based upon the assumption that some (many?) viewers rarely, if ever, bother to view documentaries or even newscasts. However, they will watch situation comedies and dramas which deal with contemporary events. (Quiz shows and music videos sometimes do so, as well.) Furthermore, as studies of Mexican soap operas (*telenovelas*), U.S. children's cartoon shows, British situation comedies, Kenyan radio plays, and

various other productions demonstrate, viewers often retain some of the more controversial information contained
in such programs. The key to success appears to be to
refrain from overloading the program with "messages" that
are "good for" the audience. Some program producers take
readily to this type of presentation, others may learn to do
so over time (if given enough time), while others either
reject it or cannot make it work. In any case, a program
schedule with nothing other than offerings containing a
large dose of "messages" almost certainly would try the
patience of many viewers and send them off to look for relief
on another channel—or even to turn the TV set off!

It has been a long-standing tradition within the electronic media that entertainment production and news
production be completely separate entities. Even the spread
of more casual news delivery styles, with their obvious
entertainment value, has not altered that tradition. On the
whole, it makes good sense: factual coverage *should* be
readily distinguishable from fictional portrayal. The famous 1938 radio broadcast of Orson Welles's adaptation of
H. G. Wells's novella *The War of the Worlds* used many
production devices associated with factual coverage of
events, such as interruptions of an entertainment program
by "news bulletins" reporting flashes of light on the planet
Mars and the landing of a large spaceship near a (real) town
in New Jersey, and an "on-the-scene" report from the
landing site in which the "reporter" sounded very much like
his real-life counterpart when the latter broadcast a live
report of the explosion of the Hindenburg zeppelin in 1937.
Panic followed, as some individuals in the general vicinity
of the "landing" flooded police stations with calls for help or
attempted to drive away from the area. Welles apologized
on the following week's broadcast, but clearly listeners felt
misled by his deliberate use of production devices associated with news coverage.

Fictional broadcasts about conflict and with direct reference to current events continue to be made, but almost always contain frequent reminders—and perhaps advance publicity—that they *are* fictional, e.g., dramas such as the U.S. *The Day After* or the British *Threads,* both of which dealt with the consequences of nuclear warfare in very graphic visual terms. Still, in many ways the line dividing television fact and television fiction seems to be growing thinner and thinner. The development of "reality-based" programs in the United States has spread to literally dozens of other countries, which often have purchased rights to use U.S. program formats for *Rescue: 911* or similar programs. Those programs claim to be based on real-life experiences, but take considerable liberty with them in order to heighten dramatic tension. They attempt to create an atmosphere of reality by using hand-held cameras, sudden loss of focus, etc., which also are characteristic of what viewers see on newscasts. So-called docudramas, where the line between established fact and speculation or outright fiction usually is unspecified, use similar production techniques, as well as footage from past TV coverage of actual events, to give their productions the aura of reality.

Docudramas and reality-based programs usually are produced by/for entertainment divisions of broadcast corporations. News divisions generally try to keep themselves as far removed as possible from such activities. However, such program formats appear to be highly popular in most countries where they are available, and they are spreading into still other markets at a rapid pace. They are a graphic indication of a widespread willingness on the part of the public to absorb and enjoy a mixture of fact and fiction. They also should remind reporters, news editors, and managers that the television-viewing public builds its impressions of society on far more than TV news reports, documentaries, interview and discussion programs, and the like. In fact, aside from the news reports and the "mini-documentary" programs such as CBS's highly popular *60 Minutes* (local versions of which also appear in many parts of the world), those other categories of informational programming attract far smaller audiences than do docudramas and reality-based shows, not to mention TV dramas and situation comedies. That is especially true for the "average" (economically, educationally) viewer.

Under such circumstances, a station or network that is serious about its commitment to reduce conflict in society and to improve coverage of ethnic minorities should consider its implementation of that commitment as an all-inclusive task. Writers, producers, directors, editors, and managers will have to coordinate their efforts when dealing with conflict and ethnic minorities. That does not mean that news and entertainment programming should become one indistinguishable mass. It means that providing more balanced images of ethnic minority life and of the causes, nature, and resolution of conflict involving minorities cannot be the task of news and public affairs divisions alone. That commitment must be led by managerial staff, which is one further argument in favor of ethnic diversity at that level, as well as at other levels, of responsibility.

During the Soviet period, broadcasters in that country, especially the national television networks, regularly showed feature films and travel and cultural documentaries from the various constituent republics. However, they presented an unrealistic, even saccharine, picture of interethnic relations and ethnic autonomy. Images of ethnic variety were scant in news and public affairs programming, which remained heavily Slavic- and Moscow-centric. Overall, Slavic anchors and newsmakers dominated the news, as did Russian, primarily Moscow, locations.

After the dissolution of the Soviet Union, many broadcast opportunities sprang up in the successor states. Now the challenge would be to represent on the airwaves the many ethnic groups *within* each new republic and to develop policies of adequate coverage in news and entertainment programs of significantly more difficult ethnic questions. Many nations already have made specific efforts to employ drama and situation comedy as vehicles for the promotion of inter-ethnic or inter-cultural harmony, although none of those efforts has involved collaboration between news and entertainment divisions. A few examples follow:

- The Canadian Broadcasting Corporation produced dramas and situation comedies such as *Les Plouffes* and *King of Kensington* which dealt with Anglo- and French Canadian relationships, usually in a comic or sarcastic manner.

- The BBC's long-running, top-rated "dramedy" (drama + situation comedy) *Eastenders* continually depicted inter-ethnic tension and harmony, with the latter almost always winning in the end.

- The writer and producers of India's highly popular soap opera *Hum Log (We People)* conceived of the series as a vehicle for encouraging "prosocial" behavior (higher status for women, greater national harmony among ethnic groups) among viewers, and regularly built appropriate messages into the plot line. Subsequent audience research studies showed some positive results.

- A Lebanese commercial TV station, CLT, frequently broadcast television plays and dramatic series which portrayed Muslim, Christian, and Orthodox families and individuals living in harmony, although that image was shattered at the outbreak of the civil war in Lebanon in 1973.

131

We do not argue that it is the job of the news and current affairs departments to become directly involved in entertainment production, or vice versa. However, it *is* the job of management to see to it that, once there is an agreed-upon commitment to heading off conflict, covering it fully and evenhandedly when it does erupt, and portraying ethnic minority experiences in more complete and balanced fashion, there will be a readiness on the part of all departments to work with each other to carry it out. The days when one could claim that viewers generally perceived television fact and fiction as two completely different entities are gone, if they ever existed. But the decreased distinction between the two can serve a positive purpose, especially in terms of exposing some audience members to material they might avoid if it were presented through informational formats.

If, as seems likely, more and more countries around the world do become multi-channel societies, there is one further issue that must be considered, as it already has been with respect to some of the new "foreign" language TV services (Arabic, Turkish) now available in Europe. How much will these additional services cost viewers? The multi-channel world of electronic media is not free: Basic monthly subscriber fees for cable or satellite services often come to U.S. $20–30 or more per month. Services above the basic level, and there are more and more of them, often add another U.S. $5–10 per month *each.* The complex and therefore expensive remote control devices needed to simplify channel selection in 100+ channel services will add yet another layer of cost.

Ethnic minorities, as noted already, often are among the least well-off groups in society. If they are to receive many of the television services that could be of some help to them—consumer advice, legal advice, ethnic minority channels—it may be necessary to consider subsidizing the reception of those services, just as some governments already subsidize housing, telephone service, heating, and other elements of life that are widely considered to be essential. Television certainly is not considered to be a luxury in most industrialized nations, any more than it is considered as just another leisure time diversion. It really is becoming an essential element in life, and it is important that the societal implications of that status be recognized.

There is nothing easy about any of the solutions proposed here, and none of them is cheap. But the implementation of even one of them seems likely to go far in helping electronic media operations which have serious commitments to presentation of material about conflict and about ethnic minorities. Each step presented here can help those operations to maintain and perhaps increase the numbers of loyal, supportive viewers and listeners in the future, even in the face of the wide range of choice offered through multichannel systems, and even without government regulation that would require *all* electronic media services to provide minimum levels of coverage of conflict and of ethnic minority material. Many studies of viewer usage of cable TV indicate that viewers soon tire of cruising through 40, 50, or more channels, and settle down to five or six for the vast majority of their viewing.

Attempts to educate and to publicize in ways similar to what we have outlined above should help to increase the odds that documentaries and serious, comprehensive, balanced newscasts stand a fair chance of being among those five or six channels. Not only will more people be exposed to societally helpful material, but also the sizes of audiences should help those operations to receive the audience shares necessary to convince the license fee-paying public, advertisers, and governments that they are worthy of investment. After all, the investment itself ultimately is in a healthier society.

# PREPARATORY DOCUMENT FOR THE COMMISSION ON RADIO AND TELEVISION POLICY

## TELEVISION NEWS COVERAGE OF MINORITIES: MODELS AND OPTIONS
### Report of the Working Group

*April 27–29, 1992*
*The Aspen Institute*
*in association with*
*The Carter Center of Emory University*

**FOREWORD**

On April 27–29, 1992, seventeen leaders and experts on television and on ethnic and racial minority groups met at the Wye River House on the Eastern Shore of Maryland to address television news coverage of minorities in both the United States and the republics comprising the Commonwealth of Independent States. This project, made possible by a grant from The Markle Foundation, was organized by The Aspen Institute's Communications and Society Program in association with the Carter Center of Emory University, as a Working Group for the Commission on Radio and Television Policy—a high level organization of 25 American and CIS television, political and academic leaders, co-chaired by former President Jimmy Carter and

Eduard Sagalaev, Vice Chairman of the Russian State Television and Radio Company–Ostankino.

The Working Group prepared a report of options for better news coverage of minorities in both areas—the United States and the CIS—with advantages and disadvantages for each of the options.

A list of participants in the Working Group follows the Report. While each contributed to the deliberations of the Report, there were no votes taken, and each person was not necessarily in agreement with each item in the Report. Accordingly, the organizers specifically disclaim attribution of any particular item to any particular participant. Co-chairs of the Working Group were Dr. Ellen Mickiewicz, Director, Commission on Radio and Television Policy, and Charles M. Firestone, Director, Communications and Society Program at the Aspen Institute. Robert Entman, Associate Professor of Communications Studies at Northwestern University was session rapporteur and co-author of the Report.

## THE REPORT

The Working Group for the Commission on Television Policy met April 27–29, 1992, to consider television news coverage of ethnic and racial minorities in the United States and in the Commonwealth of Independent States (CIS). The task was to formulate options on how television can best contribute to larger social values and goals when covering news in these two ethnically diverse societies. The options, together with an analysis of pros and cons, are forwarded to the larger Commission, which will meet in Almaty, Kazakhstan, November, 1992.

The Working Group agreed on four central social values that any television policy for covering ethnic minorities should support.

136

*First,* policy should encourage ethnic minorities to participate fully in the media life of every nation—to enable minorities to express their views to others, to enable them to fulfill the universal human need for individual self-expression, and to enable all members of the larger societies to understand the diverse peoples and experiences that compose their nations.

*Second,* policy should bolster the freedom and independence of the press. Any recommendations for alterations or additions to television's news practices are advanced with the assumption that journalistic autonomy must not be violated thereby.

*Third,* policy should serve the societies' moral values, which include most pertinently a commitment to inform all citizens, and a commitment to democracy and equal treatment of all peoples.

*Finally,* the Working Group urges the recognition that beyond these altruistic ethical goals, societies that give respectful and full voice to ethnic minorities serves the self-interests of all, including those of the ethnic majority by helping to ensure stability and forestalling the effects of pent-up frustration.

The Working Group identified three general policy goals that would help to implement these values:

1. *Increase the amount of news programming that is shaped by minority-group members and focuses on the needs and interests of minority audiences.* News that is informed by minority sensibilities can perform invaluable functions for minority communities. Seeing news from the particular ethnic perspective can enhance the self esteem and security of minority members, and provide role models to encourage members to aspire to upward mobility in society. Minority-generated programming can enhance the political interest and knowledge levels of minority members who might

otherwise withdraw from the democratic process in confused or angry alienation. As a side benefit to the larger society, such results can enhance minority groups' feelings of self confidence in dealing with majority culture, reducing hostility and misunderstanding on both sides.

2. *Provide more access within majority-oriented media for minority perspectives, consistent with the values and practices of professional and independent journalism.* The aim here is to assist both minorities in understanding themselves and their relations to the larger system, and the majority group's comprehension of its system's ethnic minorities. From the latter should spring tolerance, a new understanding of and empathy for minority groups' perspectives.

3. *Avoid stereotyping.* The Working Group believes that as a general rule it is better to cover than to suppress news; it is better to risk the wrath of certain groups or individuals who might be offended or even inflamed by a report than to engage in censorship of news. However, this general rule does not preclude a heightened sensitivity to the ways in which news can be conveyed without reinforcing painful and socially damaging ethnic stereotyping. Journalists rightly cherish accuracy; but genuine accuracy in this context means conveying complex. differentiated, and balanced portrayals of minority groups and individuals.

## PROBLEM STATEMENT

The Working Group defines "minority" strictly as consisting of ethnic and racial groups that do not constitute a numerical majority of a given CIS Republic or of the United States, or in the CIS, lack of titular status. The

138

Group recognizes that this definition leaves aside many complex issues of terminology and conceptualization. But the purposes of the Group are best served by avoiding these complexities.

Given this definition of "ethnic minority," the Group sees a number of problems to which current television practices may contribute. For example, even when accurately conveying actual events that are newsworthy by conventional standards, TV news may reinforce negative stereotypes. Standard news practices may lead TV to focus the bulk of its attention to ethnic minorities on the negative consequences of their members' actions (such as crime). TV tends to depict more positive and more frequent images of majority groups, while neglecting representatives of less powerful or powerless minority groups. Indeed, given definitions of newsworthiness, TV news may ignore smaller ethnic groups altogether unless they are involved in violence or natural disaster. Finally, typical definitions of relevant expertise and legitimate opinion may tend to exclude or underrepresent many minority views.

## OPTIONS FOR CHANGE

In recognition of these kind of problems, the Working Group devised a series of options for change in TV news practices and policies. The following are options and the advantages and disadvantages that might be attached to each. These ideas, not necessarily mutually exclusive, are grouped under the following categories content; access; management and employment; training and education; and ownership.

### A. Content

1. There should be no government censorship.

2. For coverage of ethnic crises and conflicts the following suggestions are offered:

    a. The Working Group specifically rejects the option of limiting coverage to simple, brief disclosure of facts, without commentary or detail. Although this practice is often designed to prevent television from inadvertently heightening ethnic tensions, the Group believes such an approach more often has the opposite effect. It has other negative consequences as well. Among the other outcomes of deliberate information restriction are diminishing the likelihood of comprehensive public understanding, fostering the ignorance and misunderstanding that may be the cause of the tension in the first place, and reinforcing the power of distorted rumors that may exacerbate volatile situations. The Group suggests that there are other less harmful options for media assistance in diffusing crisis situations.

    b. Develop special teams of individuals (including ethnic minorities) who will be prepared in advance for knowledgeable coverage of crises.

    c. Consult immediately leaders of those-minority groups directly involved in the crisis, for an opportunity to express views themselves on the air.

    d. Follow-up crises even after they no longer are producing breaking news, to provide deeper understanding of causes and consequences.

    e. Undertake post-crisis evaluations of coverage in order to learn from them and improve future performance.

    f. Encourage a focus on long-term trends, news that identifies problems before they become crises. Where news time is scarce, use documentaries and public affairs shows, not just regular news programs to air such reporting.

*Pros and cons for 2. b.–f.*

**Pro:** *All these options, which are not mutually exclusive, should enhance the contribution of television journalism to peaceful resolution of serious ethnic conflicts.*
**Pro:** *In addition, the suggested programming should promote general understanding among ethnic groups, whether or not there is a perceived crisis.*

**Con:** *Some of the options are expensive and may be beyond the ability of a station to implement without substantial reallocation of resources.*
**Con:** *Television organizations might focus too many resources on crisis coverage and put too little emphasis on improving normal daily news.*

3. Television organizations should make an explicit commitment to avoid ethnic stereotyping.
    a. Identify stories that reflect interaction of minorities with other groups; do not depict the group in isolation from others.
    b. Show minority members regularly in the news, not sporadically.
    c. Provide better balance of portrayal of minorities in the news. At times, it may be necessary to show people on the news, whether minority or not, in an unfavorable light. However, consistent with professional journalistic principles, journalists should avoid visual images that repeat and reinforce ethnic stereotyping (for example, using only pictures of blacks in the United States to illustrate stories about drug abuse). Where appropriate, use images of majority group members.
    d. Reflect the social diversity and variety of political views that exist among minority communities; do

not convey the false sense that all members think and live alike in every sense.

e. Multiple spokespersons should be sought from ethnic groups, rather than repeatedly quoting the same one or two ethnic representatives.

f. Ethnic group members should be covered in "soft" news, such as human interest feature stones, not just "hard" news.

*Pros and Cons for 4 a.–f:*

**Pro:** *These options are supported by scholarly research on how prejudiced thinking arises and persists. If followed, they should help to counter negative generalizations about others, among majority and minority groups alike.*

**Con:** *Television journalists may resist the options as leading to distortion of reality or treating ethnic minorities more gently than majority groups.*

4. Journalistic decisions should be based on the intrinsic significance of stories, not the availability of visual images. Attempt to develop more creative visual images and use the medium in interesting ways to illustrate stories about minorities that might otherwise be neglected for want of exciting visuals.

**Pro:** *Allowing stories to be pursued or dropped based on visual criteria invites distortion or neglect of important matters that happen not to lend themselves to visual representation.*

**Con:** *Television is a visual medium and stories that lack visual interest may not attract viewers' interest.*

5. Television organizations should establish a review group that meets regularly and includes journalists, members of minority groups, and other citizens, but not representatives of government. The group would evaluate progress in TV coverage of minorities.

> *Pro: Television journalism is a public institution and should obtain and welcome feedback from representatives of its audience.*

> *Con: Such a group could raise fears of censorship and in any case bring pressure on television organizations that compromises autonomy.*
> *Con: Audiences provide feedback on a constant basis by choosing which programs to watch and by making their views known in other ways. There is no need for such a monitoring group.*

6. Television organizations, in cooperation with schools, foundations, and other institutions, should encourage establishment of research programs on the production and reception of images of ethnic groups in the media. Television institutions should make available to researchers data on programming practices and content and (if available) audience opinions and behavior in response to programs.

> *Pro: Systematic research is the most reliable way to understand the products and effects of the media.*

> *Con: Statistics can be misused and lend a false legitimacy to discussions of complex issues where the data do not necessarily provide a good basic for conclusions.*

## B. Access

1. In order to assure fairness and reduce recriminations against television stations in dealing with minority interests, several strategies for including minority voices should be followed:
   a. Expand the roster of expert news sources and commentators to include more members of ethnic minorities.
   b. Provide more opportunities for ordinary members of minority groups to voice their views.
   c. Provide opportunities for minorities to purchase time outside of news programs to broadcast messages on television.
   d. Allocate free time outside of news programs (subsidized by government) for minority groups to voice their perspectives. Time allocated can range from one-minute messages aired over a period of time to longer documentary films.
   e. Where different languages are used by different minority members, expand programming in the languages of the minorities.

*Pro: Increases diversity of media information and sources and images.*
*Pro: Offers more opportunities for expression of minority views in members' own words*

*Con: May be expensive.*
*Con: There is no guarantee of audience interest in such programming, either among minority or majority groups, especially when funding limitations mean production quality may be low.*

2. Where there are few stations, allocate control of one broadcast channel among different ethnic groups; for ex-

ample different groups might control the station during different times of the day, or treat the channel as a common carrier facility open to all.

> ***Pro:*** *Where broadcast facilities are limited, provides greater opportunity for expression and diffusion of minority perspectives.*

> ***Con:*** *Lack of continuity and coherence in programming.*
> ***Con:*** *Potential reduction of audience size and satisfaction.*
> ***Con:*** *Number of ethnic groups may exceed available time.*

## C. Management and Employment

1. Develop explicit employment guidelines for hiring members of ethnic groups. Among the mutually exclusive options:
   a. Hiring based on percentage of workforce population of each ethnic group.
   b. Hiring based on percentage of each ethnic group in the population.

> ***Pro:*** *Gives ethnic group members direct access to the media production process and allows them to share in the selection and shaping of messages transmitted.*
> ***Pro:*** *Minimizes unconscious racism in the newsroom.*

> ***Con:*** *It may be difficult to decide how to implement the goals.*
> ***Con:*** *Limits autonomy of stations.*

   c. General goal of hiring more minority members with no specific numerical target.

*Pro: Grants stations more flexibility in hiring practices.*
*Pro: In some countries in the CIS, migration patterns may result in minority status for titular ethnic groups. Depending on unique circumstances, hiring in strict proportion to workplace or population may be less appropriate than adhering to more flexible goals.*

*Con: May lead to ineffective or unfair results.*

2. Owners should be held accountable for fulfilling ethnic hiring goals, for example by conditioning renewal of their licenses or of state subsidies (for state-owned systems).

3. It should be an explicit goal to promote minorities into management positions that provide control of key business and journalistic decisions.
  a. Top executives should be given incentives for hiring and promoting minority group members.

*Pros and cons for 2 and 3:*

*Pro: Adds teeth and incentives for stations to comply.*

*Con: May limit station's flexibility, and in the case of 2 above add a level of government regulation to their operations.*

4. Minority members should be well represented in "on-air" as well as behind the scenes journalistic decision-making positions at television stations.

*Pro: It is important for majority groups to see minorities functioning in these prestigious and powerful roles.*
*Pro: May provide another path for the entry of minority perspectives into the media messages.*

***Pro:*** *Highly visible "on-air" minority TV journalists can serve as role models and inspirations to minority members in the audience.*

***Con:*** *Putting minority faces does not solve all problems.*
***Con:*** *May produce tokenism; may falsely symbolize responsiveness to larger minority interests.*
***Con:*** *Minority members may not in fact behave differently from members of majority groups placed in similar positions and faced with similar incentives and constraints.*

5. Television stations or other entities should issue regular statistical reports to the public on employment of ethnic group members.

***Pro:*** *Provides the only systematic way to keep track of employment practices and results of attempts to hire more minority group members.*

***Con:*** *Extra paper work for TV executives.*
***Con:*** *May overemphasize hiring as a goal and cause distraction from other goals.*

6. Television industry organizations (not just stations but also production organizations, unions and other entities involved) should regularly consult with ethnic minority representatives to determine minority needs and interests, by utilizing such options as:
   a. Minority advisory boards.
   b. Minority liaison.
   c. Regular meetings with minority group leaders in the community or communities they serve.

**Pro:** *Provides a regularly updated stream of information to station owners on minority perspectives and interests that can inform programming decisions.*

**Con:** *Could degenerate into an empty bureaucratic process that distracts executives without informing them.*
**Con:** *Could serve as excuse and rationalization for not doing more than merely consulting.*

## D. Training and Education

1. Stations should create training opportunities for minority employees, such as high-level internships for junior executives, and management internships for students.

2. Television industry entities should provide support to minority college students studying journalism, as well as summer employment and internship opportunities.

*Pros and cons for 1 and 2:*

**Pro:** *Non-minorities in management and throughout the organization become more informed by minority viewpoints.*
**Pro:** *Reveals existence of options to minority members who might otherwise be unaware of career opportunities in the media.*
**Pro:** *Opens a path to high-level executive leadership by minority members.*

**Con:** *Internships may raise false expectations of rapid promotions.*
**Con:** *May create the appearance of favoritism for minorities and resentment on the part of majority group members.*

148

3. Top managers should be attentive to the need to encourage the process of mentoring (experienced senior leaders advise new minority recruits in their organizations).

*Pro: Reduces possible isolation and alienation among minority members; may speed acculturation to organization.*

*Con: Minority members may perceive overt encouragement of mentorship as paternalistic or intrusive.*

4. News programming produced for children in schools should be particularly attentive to the needs of minority children.

5. Television organizations, in cooperation with schools and other institutions, should encourage establishment of courses in media and visual literacy.

*Pros and cons for 4 and 5:*

*Pro: The output of media organizations co-exists alongside other sources of information and socialization. especially schools, which can contribute to the fulfillment of the social goals established for television.*
*Pro: Majority and minority members alike will gain information and learn how to "read " television messages in a more analytical fashion. and to convey messages more effectively on television.*

*Con: Overly didactic approaches to news programming or media literacy courses can alienate and confuse students, and undermine the legitimacy of a media source.*

6. Journalism training should include business courses.

*Pro:* *Trains aspiring journalists in other aspects of business of concern to management.*
*Pro:* *Would make trainee more effective and better prepared for assuming higher positions in industry.*

*Con:* *May overemphasize the place of business concerns in a journalistic enterprise.*

## E. Ownership

1. Create more TV stations and channels owned by and serving ethnic minorities.

*Pro:* *Gives ethnic minorities opportunities to address issues of importance to them. while serving interests of self-expression and other vital goals.*

*Con:* *Minority owners subject to economic market pressures may not act differently from majority owned stations.*
*Con:* *Potentially fragments public dialogue.*

2. Within a state-owned TV system, develop strategies such as competing independent production units that are buffered by arrangements to protect autonomy from political control.

*Pro:* *Competition in and of itself produces more information choices which may create better opportunities for covering ethnic issues.*

*Con:* *Competition for audiences can result in uniformity and avoidance of controversy.*

3. As new media and technologies develop, major efforts should be undertaken to provide control of some new outlets to minority group representatives.

> **Pro:** *Minorities would receive assured opportunity to participate in new and potentially important mass media.*
>
> **Pro:** *This is a means of providing minority ownership that would not require displacing entrenched interests.*

> **Con:** *Giving any ownership preferences to minorities raises equality of opportunity issues for members of the majority group.*
>
> **Con:** *New entrants, minority group members among them, may have limited financial resources and may therefore be weak competitors to more established firms.*

# WORKING GROUP CONFERENCE PARTICIPANTS

TELEVISION/RADIO NEWS COVERAGE OF MINORITIES:
**Models and Options
for the Commission on Radio and Television Policy**

*Wye River House
The Aspen Institute
Queenstown, Maryland
April 27–29, 1992*

PARTICIPANTS:

David Bartlett

President
Radio Television News Directors
   Association (RTNDA)
Washington, D.C.

Edith C. Bjornson

Program Officer
Markle Foundation
New York, New York

Robert Entman

Associate Professor
Department of Communication Studies
Northwestern University
Evanston, Illinois

Charles Firestone

Director
The Aspen Institute
Communications and Society Program
Washington, D.C.

Bradley S. Greenberg     Department of Telecommunications
Michigan State University
East Lansing, Michigan

Michail Guboglo     Deputy Director
Institute of Ethology and Anthropology
Moscow, Russia

Jennifer Lawson     Executive Vice President
Public Broadcasting Service
Alexandria, Virginia

Ellen Mickiewicz     Fellow
The Carter Center;
Director
International Media and Communications Program; and
Alben W. Barkley Professor of
Political Science
Emory University
Atlanta, Georgia

Andranik Migranyan     Leading Researcher
Institute of International Economic
and Political Research
Moscow, Russia

Wilhelmina Reuben-Cooke     Associate Dean for Academic Affairs
and Associate Professor
Syracuse University College of Law
Syracuse, New York

Johnathan Rodgers     President
CBS Television Stations
CBS, Inc.
Chicago, Illinois

Jorge Reina Schement     Associate Professor
Department of Communication
Rutgers University
New Brunswick, New Jersey

154

Stephen A. Sharp     Of Counsel
Patton, Boggs & Blow
Washington, D.C.

Margaret Beale Spencer     Professor
Division of Educational Studies
Emory University
Atlanta, Georgia

Jay Suber     Vice President
Features Programming;
Executive Producer
CNN Newsroom
CNN
Atlanta, Georgia

Tracy Westen     Assistant Professor
USC Annenberg School of Communi-
cations
Los Angeles, California

Mr. Sabit Zhusupov     Director
Republic Center for the Study of
Public Opinion
Almaty, Kazakhstan


*Program Coordinator:*

Ms. Catherine Clark     The Aspen Institute
Communications and Society Program
Washington, D.C.

# REPORT OF
# THE COMMISSION ON RADIO
# AND TELEVISION POLICY

November 11–13, 1992
Almaty, Kazakhstan

The Commission on Radio and Television Policy met in
Almaty, Kazakhstan on November 11–13, 1992, to consider
options and suggestions for the improvement of news coverage involving ethnic and racial minorities in both the
United States and the Republics of the former Soviet
Union. This Report reflects the discussion and sense of the
meeting, although every participant may not agree with
each point.

## Definition
The Commission defines minorities as ethnic and racial
groups that do not constitute a numerical majority in their
sovereign state, or in the case of some former Soviet republics, may comprise a majority but lack titular status.

## Underlying Values and Assumptions
The Commission's recommendations assume that the
television system will be autonomous from direct government control and censorship (even if subsidized or owned by
the State); that representation of minorities on television
will aid the understanding of both minority and majority

audiences; that it is in the self-interest of the majority to see and hear directly the expression of minority views and interests; and that the moral values of societies seeking justice will favor democracy, equal treatment of all, and the fair opportunity to hear from all sides and groups on important public issues.

## Policy Recommendations:
## Relationship to Working Group Report

The Commission considered the Report of the Working Group, which set forth an agenda of options in the areas of programming content, access, management, hiring, education, training, and ownership. The Commission's recommendations should be considered in conjunction with the Working Group Report. The following recommendations, which diverge from the sequencing of issues in the Working Group Report, reflect the pattern of discussion at the Almaty meeting.

### A. Separate Programming Versus Mainstreaming

Participants agreed that there is a need for minorities to gain access to the mass media (television, cable television, and radio) for their own issues and in their own languages. Virtually all countries attending our meeting provided descriptions of their minority language programming. This process is aided in many cases by the use of cable television and radio—often an economical and practical alternative to broadcast television. Many countries segregate this programming in separate channels of finite time periods. On the other hand, some countries augment this coverage with coverage of ethnic issues on the major news programs and channels.

The Commission agreed that both types of coverage of ethnic concerns and issues were important, but, as the Report of the Working Group states, it is critical to cover

158

minority issues on the stations with the largest audiences, in order "to assist both minorities in understanding themselves and their relations to the larger system, and the majority group's comprehension of ethnic minorities. From the latter should spring tolerance, a new understanding of and empathy for minority groups' perspectives."

However, as several participants noted, the number of minorities in any given society would make slicing up time on the main television channels simply impractical. Furthermore, the goal of attracting a large audience might well be undercut by a programming policy that simply allocates time on the largest channels to minority groups, especially when programming is provided in the minority language. A large part of the audience would surely be lost. Thus, the goal of bringing minority issues and perspectives to "mainstream" television calls for a different notion of comprehensiveness than would be the case in programming on special cable television or radio programs mainly for minority audiences in their own language.

*Recommendation No. 1:* A small portion of separated programming is insufficient. Large-audience channels and their most-watched news and public affairs programs must include within their responsibilities adequate coverage of issues relating to minorities among the viewers.

*Recommendation No. 2:* When different languages are used by minority members, the total television system should provide programming in the languages of the minorities.

In most cases, this programming would be channeled to other outlets, such as a special broadcast channel, cable television channels, or radio. The main channel or channels should nevertheless continue to provide programs on minority ethnic issues in the majority's language.

*Recommendation No. 3:* It is important for both minority and majority reporters and commentators to report stories about ethnic issues. It is equally important that more general stories be covered by reporters, some of whom are minority citizens.

*Recommendation No. 4:* To foster the understanding of minorities by majority audiences, minorities should be encouraged to make programming about their own culture for the majority audience and in the language of the majority audience.

## B. Coverage of Conflict

Perhaps the most passionate discussion was evoked by the very notion of turning the light of television on ethnic conflict itself. All of the participants noted the enormous influence of television. Some regarded that influence as vital and necessary precisely during conflict; others feared the potential incendiary effect of television coverage. Some pointed to specific outcomes they thought harmful: Sh. Medzhidov from Azerbaijan Television suggested that when the entire world is watching through the eye of the camera, this "stimulates leaders of both sides not to give in," and thus prevents compromise and retreat, and perhaps long-lasting solutions. Leonid Zolotarevsky of Ostankino Television (Channel One) drew the analogy of a family clash between husband and wife which, if it is kept in the family, has a greater probability of resolution than if the neighbors are involved. One response was that abuse of wife and children should not be concealed by observers.

In spite of those concerns, there was a strong agreement that the television public must be informed about issues of ethnic tension and conflict; as co-chair Eduard Sagalaev, head of the Confederation of Journalists' Unions, said, "no one has the right to hide information . . . we have to talk about how to report it."

President Carter, too, spoke strongly to the need to air news and to keep the public informed in all kinds of crises. "Especially in times of crisis, citizens need to know the truth. Censorship of the news media is to be rejected. It was noted that these principles in recent years have been repeatedly violated in the United States with concealment of the facts and the issuing of reports later learned to be false or misleading. During the invasions of Grenada and Panama there was an almost complete exclusion of American news media. During the Gulf War, carefully orchestrated 'news' conferences presented false pictures of pinpoint bombing and unfailing missile attacks. Most of the obfuscation was not necessary to conceal battle plans or to protect the lives and safety of military personnel. Lamentably, few news media demanded the right to inform the American public."

Oleg Poptsov, head of Russian Television, decried attempts by political authorities to limit freedom of coverage by invoking a presumed effect of this coverage on the initiation of conflict.

The issue of commentary, or summary statements made by journalists, was a point of considerable discussion. Many thought it useful and necessary to provide television viewers something more than positions of conflicting parties; the summing up of the professional journalist could add a valuable degree of understanding. Others, however, warned that precisely this commentary was likely to be subjective, biased, or ill informed. Part of the issue was professionalism: can journalists be fully professional; can they stand above the fray and be objective observers, rather than engaged participants? Can journalists in front of the camera curb a natural tendency to become actors, whose personal pronouncements may distort the report-

161

age? Will summary statements or commentary on state-owned television stations inevitably represent the views of the government, or can an independently journalistic view be heard?

Finally, several of the participants pointed to the difficulties in achieving balance when conflicts erupt. Edward Warwick, London Bureau chief for ABC News brought up the notion of "composite" coverage. While a story is breaking and reporters are on deadline, there may not be sufficient time or information available for fully comprehensive coverage. It is the responsibility of the journalist and the television station to make sure that any imbalance is righted over the course of the conflict. Similarly, balance in composite coverage was judged far preferable to the futile enterprise of attempting stories with exactly equal time or numbers of references to the conflicting parties.

The following recommendations rest on the underlying assumption that journalists should be sufficiently informed, professional, and independent to provide reports consistent with modern journalistic ethics and practices.

*Recommendation No. 1:* Television stations should not avoid serious coverage of ethnic conflict in the mistaken belief that such coverage worsens the situation. In fact, failure to explain a controversial issue fosters the ignorance and misunderstanding that may be the cause of the tension in the first place, and strengthens the power of rumors.

If the news is not conveyed by professional journalists, but by hearsay, the effects are likely to be far more dangerous.

*Recommendation No. 2:* Television journalists should, however, recognize that they have an obligation to provide their viewers with fair, accurate, and objective reporting. They should take care to explain all of the issues and positions involved in the dispute. They should carefully

162

investigate and report claims of human rights violations and atrocities, avoiding reports of unsubstantiated rumor.

*Recommendation No. 3:* In the depiction of conflict, television stations should:

a. provide a forum for spokespeople from all parties in conflict, recognizing that there may be more than two sides involved and the complexity of the conflict may call for provision of contextual material.

b. balance the more extreme voices with calm voices, and aim for peaceful resolution of the conflict. Stations should consider choosing more rational or "cool" spokespeople on a given side, rather than representatives of inflammatory extremes.

c. provide commentary only when it will help understanding. If the journalist is not sufficiently informed, professional, and independent of the government, such commentary will be regarded as reflecting the position of the government. That, in turn, may undermine the credibility of the government and the journalist among viewers.

d. commentary should always be separated from news coverage and clearly labeled, with the appropriate language, grammar and techniques of television, as commentary.

## C. Development of Longer-Range Approaches

Because conflict, by definition, unfolds rapidly and erratically, television stations often find themselves at a disadvantage, with too little preparation, too little information, and bearing too heavy a burden as the primary information source for most people. Therefore, the Commission addressed the question of how to prepare for a potential conflict that has not yet taken place, or how to treat slippage along the fault lines of social differences so that conflict may be reduced or avoided. Developing long-range approaches may seem nearly impossible while crises seem to be the norm, but "getting ahead of the curve" is no less important during times of upheaval. Perhaps most important, the Commission judged, is developing sufficient information in advance to understand and react responsibly to a conflict. To aid in the understanding of ethnic conflict, even during periods of rapid change and crisis, the television station must take responsibility for developing a longer analytic view of ethnic groups and issues. The following are recommendations of ways for stations to improve long-range coverage.

*Recommendation No. 1:* Develop a special base of knowledge including research and professionally trained analysts and prepare individuals, among them ethnic minorities, in advance of crises.

At times the use of scientific studies and recommendations can be especially helpful in (a) revealing local problems, (b) suggesting solutions to those problems, and (c) developing a specialized base of knowledge about a problem.

*Recommendation No. 2:* Identify problems before they become crises, providing direct access by minority group members, documentaries, and other programs in addition to news programs.

*Recommendation No. 3:* Avoid stereotyping of minority groups and individuals. Cover minorities in interaction with other groups. Do not always link certain ethnic groups to particular stories.

*Recommendation No. 4:* Expose and condemn attempts by governments or others to censor media during conflict situations.

## D. How Journalists Get Information
## About Ethnic Groups and Issues

From the Commission's perspective, an audience is entitled to a wide range of information from diverse sources. Because the choice of and access to information is so vital for professional coverage of ethnic groups and issues, and because, especially during times of tension and conflict, information may be in very short supply, the Commission considered the sources and practices that can best serve the journalist and the public. Meeting the audience's need for comprehensive information may well require the journalist to broaden the number and kinds of sources used and to consider very seriously the contexts of the words and pictures conveyed. The very power of pictures places a special responsibility on journalists covering violence. The Commission made the following recommendations for journalists covering ethnic groups and issues:

*Recommendation No. 1:* Expand the number of expert news sources beyond government officials.

*Recommendation No. 2:* Contact several different members of the relevant ethnic groups instead of relying always on the same spokesperson.

*Recommendation No. 3:* Choose stories for their informative content rather than sensationalist pictures.

If stations choose to use highly dramatic and sensationalist pictures, as they often will, it is imperative that the television journalist provide suitable context and perspectives to accompany and explain such images.

*Recommendation No. 4:* Establish advisory boards of ethnic and community leaders who are not representatives of the government, to meet at least quarterly with management of the television station to address and evaluate issues of coverage.

In many cases, this may be the most effective opportunity for the television station to assess its policies on these issues and to gain information from these audiences.

### E. Safety of Journalists

Increasingly, journalists covering conflict are placed in very vulnerable positions, as reports by the reporter's station may be unfavorably received by parties in the conflict and the reporter's safety placed in jeopardy.

*Recommendation:* The international community should make every effort to safeguard the lives, safety, and liberty of journalists in conflict situations. In particular, the authorities in areas of conflict should be called upon to assure access to information, freedom of movement, and protection to journalists.

### F. Employment, Education, and Training

The Commission recognizes the importance of employing members of minority groups at all levels of a television station. Members of minority groups can help the station recognize issues before they erupt into conflict and also can identify new and diverse spokespeople on ethnic and other issues.

As one Commission member put it, an integrated workforce is the best way to know who the important people are in the minority community and to provide an "early warning system" to report in a timely fashion on these issues. From a purely practical or competitive standpoint, recruiting, training, and promoting members of minority groups throughout the operations of the television station may enable the station to recognize and report stories ahead of the competition.

*Recommendation No. 1:* A high-ranking member of station management should have the responsibility for identifying and hiring minority group members at all levels of employment for both sides of the camera—editorial as well as managerial positions.

*Recommendation No. 2:* Stations should have training opportunities for minority employees and actively attract participants.

## G. Research

Though this topic is placed last in the list of recommendations concerning news coverage of minorities, the discussion of the Commission both began and ended with the need for adequate information. The need for a society to increase its fund of knowledge about its constituent parts is present in all variants of minority issues—where ethnic differences have already erupted in conflict, where minority tensions are smoldering beneath the surface calm, or, alternatively, where differences are not synonymous with conflict. And because of its centrality, information about and evaluation of television's coverage of ethnic issues is important to audiences, ethnic groups, television stations and even governments. Clearly, there is a lack of adequate information on this topic. The Commission strongly recommends expanding the base of this research.

*Recommendation No. 1:* Television stations should order regular assessments (not ratings) from independent and reliable research organizations.

*Recommendation No. 2:* Results of research should be widely shared.

*Recommendation No. 3:* Stations that have examples of successful practices of recruitment, training and/or advancement of minorities should share them. Stations also should share specific methods they have developed for covering ethnic minority or race issues. Commission members could do so by informing the Moscow or U.S. offices of the Commission, which, in turn, will inform other Commission members and wider audiences. Examples of particular problems and obstacles also should be exchanged.

**Outcomes and Future Directions**

**1.** *Television & Elections,* a publication of The Aspen Institute and The Carter Center has been published in English, French, and Russian. The Russian-language edition was prepared and distributed by the Cultural Initiative International Foundation in Moscow. The book was launched at a United Nations press conference on December 9, 1992. This book "internationalizes" the work of the first meeting of the Commission on Television Policy by relating the policy issues to the experiences of and choices made by a large variety of countries. It places the policy options in a framework applicable to any television system in the world, particularly to emerging democracies.

**2.** *Television/Radio News Coverage of Minorities,* the report of the second Commission on Television Policy, along with the Working Group Report on the same topic, will, similarly, be available as a guide for assessing options for covering these complex and difficult issues.

**3.** "Television and Changing Economic Relations: Democratization, Privatization, and New Technologies," the main agenda topic of the third Commission on Television Policy, to be held in 1993 at The Carter Center, was introduced in a special session at the Almaty meeting. Parvez Hassan, chief of the World Bank Regional Mission in Central Asia, summarized the experience of the World Bank and pointed to the critical role of television in both information and education about the process of economic reform. In addition, issues to be taken up by the 1993 Working Group and then by the Commission include the production and distribution of programming across borders, new technological developments in telecommunications, the role of government and private entities, and related questions.

**4.** *Recruitment and Training:* President Nursultan Nazarbaev of Kazakhstan and former President Carter concluded an agreement for the training of television specialists from Kazakhstan. The ABC, CBS, and NBC bureaus in Moscow and the CNN International Professionals Program in Atlanta will each accept at least one trainee from Kazakhstan. At least one of the participants from Kazakhstan will be from a minority ethnic group.

**5.** *Exchange of Programs:* An inventory of television programs for which fees will be waived was made available. These programs, mainly documentary and children's programs, represent a first step in a larger effort to make more television programs available to the former Soviet Union. It is recognized, of course, that it is always preferable for a television system to make one's own programs for one's own needs. This effort is an interim form of cooperation to supplement the products of indigenous television programmers. Together with a request form, an agreement was attached to protect the rights of the individual programs and to cycle them on to other stations making requests. It is also highly desirable to foster the wider distribution of programs from the former Soviet Union in the United States.

**6.** *Exchange of Experience:* As noted above, in the report of the Commission meeting, participants will be asked to note their experiences in minority employment and in coverage of minority issues on the news. The Moscow and U.S. offices of the Commission will collect this information, which will, in turn, be discussed at the 1993 meeting of the Commission at The Carter Center.

# COMMISSION ON RADIO AND TELEVISION POLICY

**CO-CHAIRS:**

Jimmy Carter          39th President of the United States

Eduard Sagalaev       President, Moscow Independent
                      Broadcasting Corporation; and
                      Chairman, Confederation of Journalists'
                      Unions

**MEMBERS FROM THE UNITED STATES:**

Roone Arledge         President, ABC News

Bruce Christensen     President, Public Broadcasting Service

John Danforth         Member, United States Senate

Michael Gartner       President, NBC News

Tom Johnson           President, Cable News Network
                      (CNN)

Ellen Mickiewicz      Fellow, The Carter Center;
                      Director, International Media and
                         Communications Program; and
                      Alben W. Barkley Professor of Political
                         Science, Emory University

Eric Ober             President, CBS News

Monroe Price          Professor, Benjamin N. Cardozo
                      School of Law

171

Alfred Sikes                Chairman, Federal Communications
                            Commission

Al Swift                    Member, United States House of
                            Representatives

Daniel Yankelovich          Chairman, DYG, Inc.; and
                            President, The Public Agenda
                            Foundation

**MEMBERS FROM THE NEW INDEPENDENT STATES:**

Tigran Akopyan              Chairman, State Board of Radio and
                            Television for the Republic of Armenia

Tatyana Bolshakova          Executive Director, International Asso-
                            ciation of Radio and Television (MART)

Vyacheslav Bragin           Chairman, Russian State Television
                            and Radio Broadcasting Company-
                            Ostankino

Mikhail Fedotov             Ministry of Press and Information,
                            Russian Federation

Boris Grushin               Director, Vox Populi, Public Opinion
                            Research Center; and
                            Member, Presidential Consulting
                            Council, Russian Federation

Vitaly Ignatenko            General Director, Information and Tele-
                            graph Agency of Russia (ITAR-TASS)

Bobojon Ikromov             Chairman, Television and Radio
                            Broadcasting Company of Tajikistan

Mamed Ismailov              Chairman, Television and Radio
                            Broadcasting Company, Azerbaijan

Vakhtang Khundadze          General Director, Television and
                            Radio Broadcasting Service of the
                            Republic of Georgia

Bella Kurkova               General Director, Federal Television
                            and Radio Broadcasting Service

| | |
|---|---|
| Aygar Misan | General Director, Russian Television and Radio Broadcasting Company (Moskva) |
| Sherkhan Murtaza | Chairman, Kazakh Television and Radio Broadcasting Company |
| Nikolai Okhmakevich | President, State Television and Radio Broadcasting Company of Ukraine |
| Kadyr Omurkulov | Director, State Television and Radio Broadcasting Company of the Republic of Kyrgyzstan |
| Annageldy Orazdurdyev | Chairman, National Television and Radio Broadcasting Company of Turkmenistan |
| Mikhail Poltoranin | Director, Russian Federal Information Center |
| Nugzar Popkhadze | Vice President, Moscow Independent Broadcasting Corporation |
| Oleg Poptsov | Chairman, Russian Federation Television and Radio Company |
| Imands Rakins | General Director, Latvian Television |
| Gadilbek Shalakhmetov | Chairman, Intergovernmental Television and Radio Broadcasting Company (Mir); and Vice President, Union of Journalists, Kazakhstan |
| Hagi Shein | General Director, Television Company of Estonia |
| Aleksey Simonov | Chairman of the Board, Glasnost Defense Foundation; and Secretary, Union of Cinematographers |
| Sergei Stankevich | Advisor to Russian President Boris N. Yeltsin |

Aleksandr Stolyarov     Chairman, National Television and Radio Broadcasting Company of the Republic of Belarus

Laymonas Tapinas     General Director, Lithuanian Television

Mikhail Taratuta     San Francisco Bureau Chief, Russian State Television and Radio Broadcasting Company (Ostankino)

Adrian Usaty     General Director, National Radio and Television of Moldova

Shavkat Yakhyaev     Chairman, State Television and Radio Company of the Republic of Uzbekistan

Anatoly Yezhelev     President, Telemak Television and Radio Corporation; and Chairman, St. Petersburg Union of Journalists

Tatyana Zaslavskaya     President, Russian Center for Public Opinion Research; and Member, Academy of Sciences of Russia

Yassen Zassoursky     Dean, Department of Journalism, Moscow State University; and Professor, Journalism and Literature, Moscow State University

Leonid Zolotarevsky     Director, Center for International Relations, Russian State Television and Radio Broadcasting Company (Ostankino)

# ABOUT THE AUTHORS

**Donald R. Browne** (Ph.D., University of Michigan) is professor of Speech-Communication at the University of Minnesota. His primary field of research and teaching is national and international electronic media systems—their histories, structures, audience impact, financing, and regulation. For the past several years, he has been examining indigenous languages through the electronic media in Australia, New Zealand, Canada, the United States, France, Scandinavia, Ireland, and Wales. That research centers on the representation of ethnic minorities through the media, both by themselves and by mainstream broadcasters.

**Charles M. Firestone** is Director of The Aspen Institute's Communications and Society Program. The Program is a neutral forum for public policy discourse on the impact of the communications revolution on democratic institutions and values.

After graduating Amherst College and Duke Law School, Firestone's career began as a communications attorney at the United States Federal Communications Commission, and then at a Washington, D.C. public interest law firm where he represented citizens groups from across the country before the FCC and the Federal Courts. He taught communications law at UCLA Law School for 13 years where he directed the UCLA Communications Law Program, was faculty adviser to the *Federal Communications Law Journal,* served as the first president of the Los Angeles Board of Telecommunications Commissioners, and practiced law in Los Angeles, before returning to Washington in 1990.

While in Los Angeles, Firestone also represented the League of Women Voters of California in televised statewide debates, and argued two landmark cases before the United States Supreme Court. He has written numerous articles, reports, and book chapters on communications law and policy.

**Ellen Mickiewicz,** James R. Shepley Professor of Public Policy Studies, Professor of Political Science at Duke University, Director of the DeWitt Wallace Center for Communications and Journalism of the Sanford Institute of Public Policy and Fellow of The Carter Center, is a graduate of Wellesley College and received her doctorate from Yale University. Her book, *Split Signals: Television and Politics in the Soviet Union* (1988, Oxford University Press), was given the Electronic Media Book of the Year award by the National Association of Broadcasters and the Broadcast Education Association. She is the author or editor of five other books, and her articles have appeared in such journals as *American Political Science Review, Public Opinion Quarterly, Slavic Review,* and *Journal of Communication,* and newspapers such as *The New York Times* and *Corriere della Sera.* She has been interviewed for network television news and public radio and television broadcasts, including the *MacNeil-Lehrer News Hour.*

She is Director of the Commission on Radio and Television Policy of Duke University and The Carter Center of Emory University. Dr. Mickiewicz has served as advisor to the Council for International Exchange of Scholars, and to the Kennan Institute of the Woodrow Wilson Center. She is a member of the Council on Foreign Relations and was President of the American Association for the Advancement of Slavic Studies.

# ACKNOWLEDGMENTS

We would like to acknowledge the assistance of Marc Berenson, Edith Bjornson, Mimi Choi, Cathy Clark, Katharina Kopp, Kelly Nugent, and W. Daniel Wright. Jeffrey Brand, Robert Entman, Bradley Greenberg, Lidia Polskaya, Leila Vasilieva, and Sabit Zhusupov contributed additionally to this work through their research papers prepared for the Working Group. We thank again Robert Entman for serving as rapporteur and co-author of both the Working Group and Commission reports. Support for this work was given by the John and Mary R. Markle Foundation.